Isadora E. Mathews

1954

IN THE STEPS OF JESUS

Travel Books by H. V. Morton

IN THE STEPS OF JESUS

By H. V. MORTON

ILLUSTRATED WITH PHOTOGRAPHS

NEW YORK · 1953

DODD, MEAD & COMPANY

915.694
m889i

132483

ILLUSTRATIONS

ILLUSTRATIONS

INTRODUCTION

I

This book is based on my *IN THE STEPS OF THE MAS-TER* and I have prepared it for family reading. I have done this with great pleasure, because I think that a book of this kind would have helped answer many of the questions we were in the habit of asking in our family.

For something like sixteen hundred years pilgrims have been visiting the land in which Jesus was born and in which He died. They have gone there to see for themselves such places as Bethlehem, Nazareth, Galilee and Jerusalem, and many have hoped that walking literally in the steps of Jesus, they might draw nearer to Him in spirit.

It has been truly said that the best guide to the Holy Land is the Bible, and one of the great experiences of travel there is to see the habits and customs of long ago perpetuated in the life of today. But within modern times great changes have taken place and for the first time in their history the Bible lands have met the impact of modern ideas and inventions. Many ancient ways of life are naturally fated to disappear, and those of us who have been privileged to travel about the country before change swept too much away are indeed fortunate. At the moment the period of transition has many incongruous aspects. Women still trim their lamps as in the parable of the Foolish Virgins within the shadow of great hydro-electric power schemes, and transcontinental air liners swoop down on the airport of Lydda above the heads of caravans which might be moving out of *Exodus* into *Deuteronomy*.

It is, however, with a thrill that the traveler still sees the camel and the ox yoked together, illustrating the words of St. Paul, "be ye not unequally yoked with unbelievers," or the gardener kicking away the earth rampart of an irrigation channel and letting loose a stream of water ("thou sowedst the seed, and wateredst it with thy foot") and everywhere the shepherd coming over the stony hills like the Good Shepherd carrying a lamb across his shoulders.

It is impossible to travel for a day in the Holy Land without recalling some verse or incident in the Bible, and it may well be that an obscurity which has defeated the student at his desk may suddenly be illuminated on the roadside.

In no way is a journey to the Holy Land more valuable than in giving us a clear idea of the background of the New Testament. It is remarkable to realize in how small a country Jesus conducted His ministry, and that when He was farthest away from Jerusalem, on the borders of Tyre and Sidon, He was never more distant from the capital than what to a modern man would be a few hours' journey in a car. The faith that conquered the Roman Empire and created the modern world was born in a country no larger than the state of Massachusetts.

To have walked the walls of Jerusalem, to have explored its streets, to have rambled over the Mount of Olives to Bethany, and back again along the dusty road, is to see the events of the Gospel story with new eyes. When I stood upon the Mount of Olives and saw before me the city of Jerusalem lifted on its rocky shelf, with the huge mosque of the Dome of the Rock, resembling so strongly the Temple of Herod which it replaced, many aspects of the last Passover and the Crucifixion, and the movements of the chief actors during that time, were made clear to me.

Study of the Gospels has not perhaps been assisted by that frame of mind which regards them as verbally sacred. This was an attitude more often encountered, I fancy, in my childhood than today. I can still remember the crushing retort of a teacher in my young days when I asked with a sincere and reverent thirst for knowledge how artists know that Jesus wore a beard. For some reason which has never been clear to me, this was considered an irreverent question. I was made to feel almost like a blasphemer and of course my questions became fewer. As I grew up I came to realize that there is a kind of devotion which excludes any kind of inquiry or criticism. To such people the events described in the Gospels might have taken place not on this earth, but in some hushed, stained-glass country where nothing is real. The truth is, of course, that the Gospels are bursting with life. They are full of noise and dust and thirst, of busy market places, of angry crowds, of invalids dragging their deformed bodies about the countryside, as people still do today in the East, of thieves and crooks and agitators, of superior persons and proud persons. Indeed, few narratives have come down to us from the ancient world more full of the bustle and smell of common life than the four Gospels.

While it is true that the eye of faith may be more pene-

trating than the human eye, and that belief may lead more
surely to knowledge than learning, my mind is such that I
have always wanted to know the facts, if possible, and in this
book I have treated the subject of the Crucifixion as a historical event, like the Magna Charta or the Battle of Gettys-
burg, which can be tested by evidence. And this is so, of
course. Jesus lived within a by no means remote historical
period. The Pyramids were already hoary with antiquity
when He was born. As ancient historians reckon time, He
was born only yesterday.

Scholars believe that Jesus was born during the reign of
Augustus Caesar, in the year B.C. 2, and that He was cruci-
fied in the reign of Tiberius, on Nisan (April) 14, in either
A.D. 29 or 30.

The chief literary witnesses to the life of Jesus are the
four Evangelists, Matthew, Mark, Luke and John. No documents in the world have been subjected to more minute
textual, and other, scrutiny than the Gospels. Critics now
date them, approximately, as follows.

St. Mark: written about A.D. 60.
St. Matthew: "   "   A.D. 70.
St. Luke: written between A.D. 75-85.
St. John: "   "   A.D. 80-110.

The four canonical Gospels relate either the impressions
and recollections gathered from eye witnesses who had
known Jesus in the flesh, or else they embody recollections
written by those who had personally been with Him.
Whole libraries have been written on the authorship of the
Gospels by scholars who have examined and analyzed the
documents from every possible angle.

St. Mark's Gospel, the earliest of the four, is believed to have been composed about thirty years after the Crucifixion by one who had either known Jesus or had heard of Him possibly from the lips of St. Peter. The writer is by many believed to be John Mark, who is mentioned in *Acts* XII, verse 12, and whose mother, Mary, had a house in Jerusalem which may have been the scene of the Last Supper. The earliest Christian tradition states that this Gospel represents the reminiscences of St. Peter, and it has been conjectured that Mark, his companion, wrote down all St. Peter had told him about Jesus after the Apostle had been martyred in Rome.

St. Matthew was identified in early times with Matthew or Levi, a publican or customs official, who gave up his post in Galilee to follow Jesus. This is not now widely believed by scholars. The modern view is that the writer was an unknown Christian Jew who used the already existing Gospel of St. Mark and added to it other material, some of which may have been provided by Matthew.

St. Luke, whose Gospel was described by Ernest Renan as "the most beautiful book in the world," was also the author of the *Acts of the Apostles*. St. Paul refers to him in his *Epistle to the Colossians* as "Luke, the beloved physician," and attempts have been made to prove, by an analysis of the words he used, that he was a Greek doctor. No criticism has been able to shake the traditional view that Luke was a Greek Christian who was present with Paul at certain points in his travels and was with him in Rome.

The authorship of St. John's Gospel has inspired an enormous amount of critical literature. The author would appear to have been an eyewitness to many of the most important events he describes. He was apparently present at the Last Supper and at the Crucifixion, and later he saw the Risen Lord. The tradition is that he was John, son of Zebedee, who in his old age at Ephesus committed his reminiscences to writing.

II

No country in the world has changed in a more rapid and spectacular manner in modern times than the Holy Land.

When the first World War broke out in 1914, Palestine and Syria had been part of the Turkish Empire since the Crusades. They were ruled from Constantinople by the Sultan of Turkey, and Christian travelers were not always welcome there.

It was hoped by the Allies that Turkey would remain neutral in 1914 but that was not to be. She declared war on the side of Germany. When this happened a British army was sent to Palestine and eventually drove the Turks out of the country. So, for the first time since the Crusades, a Christian nation ruled Palestine.

When the War was over the League of Nations placed Palestine under British rule, and a country which for centuries had shared the inertia of the Turkish Empire was suddenly galvanized into activity. If we may think of Palestine as the Sleeping Beauty, we must imagine her awakened not by one prince but by three, a Briton, an Arab and a Jew!

The awakening was by no means pleasant, and many Palestinians began to wish that they had been allowed to go on slumbering under the Turks.

The trouble was that during the war Britain had given two pledges, one to the Arabs, who had assisted her against the Turks, and one to the Jews. The Arabs believed that with British help they would be allowed to make Palestine into an Arab state, and the Jews had been promised that with British help a "National Home" for Jews all over the world would be created in Palestine. Foreign Jews began to come into the country to make their homes there, and to buy up Arab land, and so Jew and Arab were set against each other and both of them turned against Britain.

The origin of Britain's promise to the Jews is interesting. It grew out of a dangerous war-time shortage in the manufacture of explosives. In those days wood alcohol was a necessary ingredient in the manufacture of cordite, and in 1916 the German submarines were making it impossible for Britain to import enough timber for this purpose from the United States. Therefore British scientists were ordered to experiment in the hope that some substitute for wood alcohol might be found. There was at that time a brilliant, and then unknown, Jewish professor of chemistry at Manchester University named Dr. Chaim Weizmann who promised that he would work day and night until the difficulty had been overcome. In a few weeks he announced that the problem had been solved, and thus the British supply of cordite was assured.

When asked what honor or reward he would like, Dr. Weizmann replied that he desired nothing for himself. The great wish of his life was to see a National Home for the Jews in Palestine, and all he asked was that if Britain won the war she would view this possibility with favor.

So it came about that when Britain began to rule Palestine after the first World War, she did her best, but without success, to be fair to both sides. The Jews introduced thousands of colonists into the country, and much of the best land came into their possession. There was much talk of splitting the country into halves, one Jewish and the other Arab, but such a small land was not really capable of partition. The result was that when the British Mandate ended in 1948, the Jewish State of Israel was at once proclaimed, with the clever chemist, Dr. Chaim Weizmann, as its first President, a position he held until his death in 1952. The Arabs immediately made war. They invaded Israel from Syria and Lebanon on the north, Irak and Jordan on the east and Egypt on the south. The war dragged on for months until, under the auspices of the United Nations, a truce was arranged in 1949 under four separate armistice agreements, and even now, four years later, these have not yet been translated into peace.

The little state of Israel is still surrounded by potential foes and its frontiers are those which existed at the time of the truce. The Jordanian Arabs hold Jericho, Bethlehem, the old city of Jerusalem and half the Dead Sea; the Egyptians hold a small strip of coast south of Gaza. As feeling still runs high between Jews and Arabs, these frontiers make it extremely inconvenient for the traveler who is not allowed to pass freely from Jewish territory into Arab territory, and vice versa. No doubt these frontiers will be subject to change some day but how long it will be before the visitor to the Holy Land will be able to pass easily from Dan to Beersheba, as he was able to do under British rule, it is impossible to say. The Republic of Israel occupies about 8,000 square miles of a total of about 10,400, which

16 .

is the area of Palestine. The population is said to be about 1,370,000, of whom 1,200,000 are Jews, mostly immigrants from other countries. The state is governed by an Executive Council appointed by the President and by a parliament, called the Gnesset Israel, of a hundred and twenty members. The official language of the country is Hebrew.

In their first invasion of Palestine under Moses, and in their second invasion under Dr. Weizmann, the Jews have faced many difficulties. The Arab still regards himself as the original inhabitant with a historical title to the land; and it remains to be seen whether he will make terms with the children of Israel who have emerged from the inhospitable deserts of Europe, bringing with them the ways and the marvels of the modern world.

IN THE STEPS OF JESUS

CHAPTER ONE

*Describes a journey to the Holy Land and an impression of
Jerusalem. I visit the Holy Sepulcher, the Mount of Olives,
the Garden of Gethsemane and the ghost of Solomon's
Temple.*

§ 1

As the sun was setting over Egypt I stepped into a little
boat on the Suez Canal. The water that fell from the oars
was red, but before I had crossed the narrow canal to El
Kantara it was silver, and the moon was shining. The little station was silent and deserted among the sandhills.
Moonlight silvered the rails that ran north across the Sinai
Desert into Palestine, and all around was a green stillness
stretching out into far spaces under the stars.

The minutes slipped into hours as I waited for the train
to Jerusalem. But I liked waiting there, listening to the
queer sounds of the night, the distant barking of dogs in
the desert, the harsh grumbling of camels as they crouched
in the moonlight of the station yard.

The train, when it arrived, lay for a long time in the
station, as if working up enough courage for its nightly
plunge into the sand. Then it slipped away from El Kantara and went out into the moonlight.

In the morning I looked out of the window and saw,
moving high on an embankment and outlined against the
sky, a file of burdened camels plodding slowly into the

dawn. And I knew that in this brief flash, before the train went past, I had seen the spirit of this road: for the railway to Jerusalem follows an ancient route. It runs over the ageless caravan road to and from Egypt, and it was along this road that Joseph was led into captivity. It was the road over which the first great Jewish financier, Solomon, sent his sandalwood and his spices to the markets at Memphis. It was a road that led everywhere: to Damascus in the north, to the desert city of Petra in the east, to Egypt in the south.

On the same embankment I saw some Arabs muffled and shrouded in the cold air. First came a donkey with a woman and a child upon its back and behind them strode a man. And I remembered again that this was the way Joseph and Mary fled with a Child into Egypt.

The train climbs so slowly that Arab boys run beside it, holding bunches of red anemones which they offer to the passengers. The mountains are scorched and brown. The roads are white ribbons that slip in and out of the hills. Camels, absurdly large, draw diminutive plows sullenly and, it seems, reluctantly, over the meager fields. Families who might be on a journey from *Deuteronomy* to the *Book of Kings* walk behind laden donkeys; here and there a fine old patriarch, who reminds one of Abraham, leans on his staff to watch the daily train go past.

As the train climbs and winds into the hills toward the mountain capital of Jerusalem, you are aware of something fierce and cruel in the air. Judea is fiercer than anything in Europe. It is a striped, tigerish country, crouched in the sun, tense with a terrific vitality and sullen and dispassionate with age.

The fierceness of the parched gullies, the harshness of the barren hilltops, the passion of the caked earth where lizards dart and flash, and the burning cruelty of waterless valleys, are concentrated and made visible upon the highest of the hills. And the name of this materialization is Jerusalem.

§ 2

I went to a hotel not far from the Jaffa Gate where an Arab, who was dressed like a Turk in a musical comedy, carried up my bags. An Armenian registered me. A German chambermaid unlocked my bedroom door.

It was an attractive room with a writing table and a good light over the bed, and it had a little balcony overlooking a narrow street and the walls of a convent school. Through the windows I could see the nuns moving about a large, bare dormitory, making two rows of little beds.

I went straight out to find my way to the Church of the Holy Sepulcher. I had been studying a street plan of Jerusalem for weeks, and wondered whether I could find my way alone through the twisting lanes of the old city. As soon as I appeared in the Jaffa Road I was surrounded by eager, whispering men, wearing European suits and the red tarbush which used to be the sign of Turkish citizenship.

"You come with me to the Holy Sepulcher!" they whispered. "I show you everything!"

There seemed to me to be a definite blasphemy in their invitations, so I shook them off and went on alone. They followed me like figures in a nightmare, whispering, and once even daring to pull me by the sleeve. I had to make

· 23

it very clear that I disliked them before they disappeared from sight. I was distressed to find that the real Jerusalem, full of donkeys and camels and men selling oranges, was very different from the clear street plan that I knew by heart! I came to the Jaffa Gate and saw a great sweep of the city wall running to the south. I passed in and entered the old city. I saw to my right the huge, square tower, known as David's Tower, which is in reality all that is left of Herod's great tower, Phasael. I saw it with the emotion which any relic of the time of Christ must inspire, whether the observer be a devout Christian or merely a devout historian. Those huge yellow stones at the base of the tower existed in the Jerusalem of the Crucifixion. Perhaps His eyes saw them.

Around this tower and near the Gate surged an extraordinary crowd, which seemed to me, so newly from the West, to be a perfect microcosm of the East, and I looked at it with the delight of a child at a Christmas circus.

I could distinguish peasants from the villages, the *fellahin,* born farmers and plowmen, who are a queer mixture of cunning, simplicity and violence. I remembered a story someone once told me about the Palestinian *fellah.* It was that God, at the making of the world, sent out His angel with the gift of Intellect, and gave to each man his share. There were no complaints. He then sent out the angel with the gift of Fortune. And every man grumbled. He followed this with the world's allowance of Stupidity, and the angel, carrying this gigantic burden, encountered the *fellah,* to whom he had already given his dole of intellect and fortune.

"O angel," said the *fellah,* "what is it you bring this time?"

"O *fellah,* it is Stupidity!" said the angel.

"O angel," cried the *fellah,* greedily, "give me the lot, because I am a poor man with a large family!"

So the angel gave him the world's stupidity.

It is an unkind story, but I feel that it could not have been composed about anyone who was not, in spite of everything, rather simple and decent.

Then, distinct from the *fellah,* was the Bedouin Arab. Although he walks in rags, he moves like a king of the earth. He despises the *fellah* and his spade. The Bedouin is a man of ancestry and freedom, of flocks and herds, and tents which he calls "houses of hair." In him Abraham lives on into the modern world.

There were the town Arabs in European clothes and tarbushes. There were Armenians, Franciscan friars, and white Dominicans. There were Greek priests, who are square-bearded like Assyrian kings and stride through the crowd wearing rusty cassocks and high round black hats. Strangest of all were the queer old Jews with their long, straggling beards, and curls of hair tapping against their temples. Arabs sat dreamily under the awning of a café, sucking at hookahs; others, strung up to a high pitch of excitement, expended in the purchase of a handful of dates, or a lettuce, more passion than a westerner expends in a month.

In spite of all my maps and plans I confessed myself hopelessly lost in this bright chaos, but I walked on with resolution, knowing that if I appeared to hesitate for one instant a pack of guides would be on my heels. But it was not a pleasant feeling because, when I had left the crowd behind, I found myself in dark, narrow lanes faced with scabrous walls, broken only by dark openings to cellars or to dank little courtyards into which cats darted with the speed and terror of wild animals. The thought crossed my mind that anyone who ventures alone into these lanes without a knowledge of Arabic deserves a knife in the back. But, miraculously it seemed to me, I came to a crossroad where donkeys were plodding along with sacks of wheat for the grindstone. I looked up and read on a blue plate let into the wall, *Via Dolorosa.*

"If I follow this," I thought, "it is bound to lead me to Calvary, which is inside the Holy Sepulcher."

And no sooner had I thought it than I felt ashamed of my thought. I had blundered on the Way of the Cross and I had treated it as if it were any ordinary street. I felt ill at ease. I set this down because it is so typical of one's first thoughts in Jerusalem. The mind, accustomed to the divine Christ of western churches, encounters in Jerusalem the memory of Jesus the Man, the Jesus who ate and slept and became weary, who drove the hucksters from the Temple, who drank the cup of death on Golgotha. At home one always thinks of Jesus in heaven, on the right hand of God the Father, but in Jerusalem one thinks of Him walking the dusty white roads, and one's intelligence is perpetually rejecting or accepting certain places that tradition associates with His manhood. As God, He is everywhere, but in Jerusalem centuries of piety have competed to place His footsteps on this stone and that road. It was almost with a shock that I realized that the *Via Dolorosa* could be a real road with men and women and animals upon it.

I do not know for certain whether the *Via Dolorosa* is really the road on which Jesus carried the Cross, and neither, I think, does anyone else. Its route depends on the situation of Pilate's judgment hall and the unknown position of the Gate Genath. But it does not seem to me to matter very much whether it is the actual road or a memorial to the actual road. What is important is that men and women who have walked upon it have met there the vision of Christ.

The *Via Dolorosa* led to a gate in a wall. On the other side was a large courtyard steeped in the morning sun. It was quiet and peaceful after the crowded lanes outside. At the far end rose up the fine façade of the Church of the Holy Sepulcher, which is today almost as the Crusaders left it. A stone seat runs along one side of the courtyard. I sat there for a moment and watched the people going in and coming out in the church.

They were the strangest people. There were monks wearing white habits and khaki sun hats. There were Arab women. There were incongruous parties from cruising steamers, shepherded by hustling, irreverent guides, and there were several old shepherds in sheepskin jackets and patched-up rags, who reverently removed their slippers in the courtyard and walked into the church barefoot. How interesting this was for I remember that the Jews used to go barefoot into Solomon's Temple and the Moslems today remove their slippers in the mosque, and here were native Christians observing the same custom.

I noticed that just inside the porch of the church, to the left hand as you go in, was a wooden divan spread with carpets and cushions. On this reclined a calm, aristocratic-looking man with a neatly trimmed beard, a turban, and a long black robe. He was one of the Moslem doorkeepers to whose family the task of locking up the Holy Sepulcher had been entrusted by Saladin eight hundred years ago.

The Tomb of Jesus Christ is a small cell lined with marble, six and a half feet long, and six feet wide. Only two or, at the most, three people can enter at one time. On the right hand is a cracked slab of white marble, three feet in height, covering the rock on which He was placed after the Crucifixion.

From the marble roof of this tiny cell hang lamps which belong in various proportions to the Greek, Latin, Armenian and Coptic Churches. The Roman Catholics are known in Palestine as the Latins. Standing at the head of the marble slab was an impassive Greek monk with a soft-spade-shaped black beard. He wore a black cassock and a high, black, rimless hat, beneath which his hair was pinned at the back in a round bun. He held a bunch of candles in his hand and, as the pilgrims entered, gave one to them, which they lit from others burning in the tomb.

I could see a pilgrim kneeling at the sepulcher, so I waited in the small, dark antechamber outside.

Becoming impatient, I bent down and, peeping through the low entrance, saw that the man inside was an old, bent peasant in ragged clothes, his feet in a pair of huge shoes made of felt. He was a Bulgarian who had come over in a pilgrim ship, as the Russians used to come, and he had probably been saving up all his life for that moment.

He was kneeling at the marble slab and kissing it repeatedly, while tears ran down the deep wrinkles of his face and fell on the stone. His large, rough hands, the nails split and black with labor, touched the marble gently with a smoothing motion; then he would clasp them in prayer and cross himself.

He prayed aloud in a trembling voice, but I could not understand what he was saying. Then, taking from his pocket various pieces of dirty paper and a length of ribbon, he rubbed them gently on the Tomb and put them back in his pocket.

I thought there might perhaps be room for me, so I bent my head and entered the Sepulcher. The Greek monk, the kneeling peasant and myself quite filled the small space. And it would have been all right if the old man had continued to kneel, but, disturbed perhaps by my entrance, he rose up, the tears still falling, and whispered something to me. We were now standing, our chests touching, and, looking into his eyes, I saw that I was looking at real happiness.

This was his life's dream. I had never seen such happiness before. Never in all my life have I beheld peace and contentment written so clearly on a human face. I would have given the world to have been able to speak to him, but we stood there in the Tomb of Christ, he whispering something to me which I did not understand, and I shaking my head.

He then turned from me toward the Greek monk and said the same thing to him. But the monk could not understand, and he also shook his head. The old man became frantic with anxiety. He raised his voice slightly and then, casting a swift glance toward the marble slab, lowered it, and pointed to his forehead and to the lamps that hang over Christ's Tomb. Then the monk understood. Nodding gravely, he lowered one of the lamps on a chain and taking a piece of cotton wool, he dipped it lightly in the oil of the lamp, and with this made the sign of the Cross upon the peasant's face.

The old man sank down on his knees and turned again to the Tomb, unwilling to leave, incoherent with faith and devotion, his big scarred hands touching the marble lovingly as if stroking the hair of a child. Presently he backed out of the candlelight into the dim Chapel of the Angel.

§ 3

As I went on through the old city, I was conscious of a feeling of imprisonment. All the dark little lanes, the high, blank walls, and the jumbled buildings erected to the glory of God, are bound tightly together by a high city wall. The wall of Jerusalem, her armor and shield in time of trouble, still exerts a powerful influence on the mind and you are subconsciously aware of it every minute of the day. You are either inside the wall, acutely aware of its encircling embrace, or you are outside it, looking back at it, thinking that it clasps the city in its brown stone arms as if trying to shield it from the modern world.

I came by way of narrow street and blank wall, by sunlight and by shadow, to the ancient Gate of St. Stephen. I saw, framed in the graceful Saracenic arch of its stones, a brilliant little picture of the world beyond the wall. I sighed with relief at the sight of so much air and openness, so much sky, and mountains with the sun over them. And the hillside that rose up opposite was the Mount of Olives.

All my life I have had a picture of the Mount of Olives in my mind, a picture composed by my own imagination and influenced by illustrations in books and by canvases in art galleries; but it was a very different picture from the reality. I had always thought of the Mount of Olives as an improbable hill, with plenty of tall cypress trees among belts of woodland and little gardens with wells and fountains in them. But the real Mount of Olives is a bare ridge sloping up from the stricken-looking Kedron Valley; a ridge of rock on which the sun beats down all day long. There are white tracks twisting here and there among the rocks, and a few plowed fields terraced in the rock and upheld on the hill by breast-high walls of limestone. In these fields are a few stumpy olive trees.

In any other place the Mount of Olives would seem bare and inhospitable, but, in contrast to Jerusalem and the mountains by which it is surrounded, it is peaceful and gracious; the only place in which today, as in the time of our Lord, you could go to sit under a tree and forget the nervous tension of the city.

Low down, just where the Jericho Road sends a branch road right up over the crest of the Mount of Olives, is a small patch of trees within a wall. I looked at it with the emotion it must always inspire. It was the Garden of Gethsemane.

When I came out of St. Stephen's Gate, I saw that the whole length of the eastern wall of Jerusalem overhangs a rocky gorge. The sloping ground outside the wall is covered with countless thousands of Moslem tombs; opposite on the slopes of the Mount of Olives are the Jewish tombs. Their white stones shine like bones. Both Jews and Moslems believe that the Last Judgment will be held in the arid Valley of the Kedron, between Jerusalem and the Mount of

Olives. As I looked at the tombs, and then at the grim city wall, it seemed to me that Jerusalem, so cruel in appearance, so uncompromising, had, like an ogre, devoured these thousands of dead and had cast their bones over the ramparts to rot and bleach in the sun.

The road leads down into the Kedron Valley. It is white and dusty and low stone walls hem it in. It runs straight through the valley and down to Jericho and the Dead Sea. But the branch road to the left leads over the Mount of Olives to Bethphage and Bethany. And this is the road I walked, with the sun beating on it and the heat quivering like white fire on the rocks.

I looked back from the depths of the Kedron Valley, but I could see only the tawny wall of Jerusalem towering above me on its rocky platform. As I began to climb the Mount of Olives, first a minaret, then a dome or two, appeared above the wall. Near the top of the Mount the whole city lay before me, slightly tilted in the direction of the Mount of Olives like an immense relief map that was slowly sliding into the abyss of the valley.

My first thought was amazement that Jerusalem should ever have been built. A more unlikely place for a famous city cannot be imagined. The arid mountains lie about it, rolling in long brown ridges against the sky, and in the valley below is only one spring of water—the Fountain of the Virgin. Jerusalem's water comes today, as it did in Old Testament times, from Solomon's Pools near Hebron. Water is also pumped from Ain Fara, the traditional "still waters" of the twenty-third Psalm. Today, as in olden times, every drop of rain that falls on this high mountain

Christ's body, removed from the cross, was laid on the stone shelf where the priest rests his hands.

A procession in the Via Dolorosa in Jerusalem has followed Christ's path to the Crucifixion place where the Holy Sepulcher Church now stands.

ridge is saved in deep rock cisterns. There is a splendid defiance about the situation of Jerusalem, or perhaps it would be more correct to say that no people who did not believe themselves to be in the special care of God would have dared to have built a city in defiance of all the laws of prudence.

And my second thought was that never had I seen a more intolerant-looking city. All the hardness of the rock and the smoldering fires within the rock seemed to have boiled up out of the bowels of the earth and cooled into the city of Jerusalem. It was a perfect expression, so it seemed to me, of the cruelty and the fierceness of the Judean highlands. This high city, perched above ravines and lying among the debris of centuries, might, it seemed, be the abode not of men and women and children, but the dwelling place of ruthless emotions such as Pride and Arrogance and Hate. And as I sat for a long while looking down on Jerusalem, I thought to myself: "That is undoubtedly the place that crucified Jesus Christ." Like an echo to my thought came a terrible reply: "And it would probably do so again."

The longer I looked at Jerusalem, the more I felt convinced that my first impression was not overdrawn or extravagant. If Jerusalem has not been born out of volcanic lava, she has at least been born from the fire of men's mind. Splendid and terrible things have happened behind her walls. The modern world was born in their shadow. Strange that the greatest event in the history of Mankind should have occurred on this bare plateau; stranger still, perhaps, that Jerusalem should still wear her historic air of intolerance. I seemed to hear a Voice in the pulse of the heat, and the Voice said:

"O Jerusalem, Jerusalem, thou that killest the prophets, and stonest them which are sent unto thee, how often would I have gathered thy children together, even as a hen gathereth her chickens under her wings, and ye would not!"

The words beat against my brain like an echo of the heat that quivered above the Mount of Olives. I listened again, but there was no sound but the thrusting of a plow through the dry soil and the click of a mule's hoof against a flint.

§ 4

If you asked me to point out the most surprising sight in Jerusalem I would not say the Tomb of Christ or any of the well-known Christian holy places but a huge open space at the southeast angle of the city walls known as the Dome of the Rock. This is, after Mecca, the most sacred mosque in Islam.

It occupies the place where the Temple of Solomon once stood. This great temple, with its Holy of Holies and the Ark of the Covenant, was destroyed in 586 B.C. when the Israelites were carried into bondage in Babylon. Fifty years later it was rebuilt after a fashion, but those who remembered the old Temple could not see it without tears. It was not as splendid as its predecessor, and many of the sacred objects had been lost or destroyed during the exile, including the Ark of the Covenant. What happened to this has never been known.

It was Herod the Great who conceived the ambitious idea of rebuilding Solomon's Temple. He was a great

architect and the fine new buildings which he gave to
Jerusalem must have made the Temple look shabby and
old-fashioned. He started the rebuilding in the winter of
20 B.C. and the work went on throughout his lifetime and
long after his death. All through the life of Jesus workmen were busy on the Temple, and every time He came
up to Jerusalem He must have seen them employed on
some part of the enormous sanctuary. Herod's Temple
was not finally completed until thirty-four years after the
Crucifixion. And eight years after, when the Romans put
down a Jewish revolt, it disappeared in flames forever.

For hundreds of years this immense open space remained
a ruin in Jerusalem. When the Arabs invaded the country
in 635 A.D. it was a gigantic dunghill where all the refuse
of the city was dumped. The Arabs decided to clean it up
and make a great mosque there and that is the building
we see today.

I have called it the most surprising sight in Jerusalem because this mosque follows in general outline the shape of
Herod's Temple. I suppose when the Arabs cleared away
the rubbish thirteen hundred years ago, and uncovered the
gigantic platform on which the Temple had once stood, it
was simpler to follow the lines of the ancient buildings than
to make something new. So it might be said that the ghost
of Herod's Temple exists today in Jerusalem, the Temple
in which Jesus preached, and from whose courts he drove
the merchants and the hucksters.

Seven great gates pierce the massive walls that enclose
the Mosque. When I entered I found myself in silence and
in spaciousness. The Temple area is like a gigantic stone-
paved park in the center of a congested city. My first im-

· 35

pression was of acres of flagstones edged with grass stretching onto higher levels and bounded by shady colonnades. In the center of the open space was the shrine of the Dome of the Rock, erected over the rock which is believed to have stood beneath the Jewish altar of burnt offerings.

Before I entered any of the buildings I sat down and tried to get a general idea of the place, but all the time I found myself looking not at the present-day Moslem sanctuary but at the older Jewish Temple which it has replaced. The resemblance is astonishing. For instance, the sheiks of the mosque, who trim the lamps and sweep and tidy up the place, lock the doors and perform all kinds of services, live in quarters under the colonnades of the mosque just as the priests of Solomon's Temple used to do. Like them, they have regular terms of office, on the completion of which they return home to wait until their time of ministration arrives again. This is exactly what used to happen in the Temple of the Jews. We learn in *St. Luke* how Zacharias, the aged father of John the Baptist, received a vision in the Temple "while he executed the priest's office before God in the order of his course." The "course" was a week's continuous service reckoned from Sabbath to Sabbath. "When the days of his ministration were fulfilled," says St. Luke of Zacharias, "he departed unto his house."

Not ten yards from me, in the shade of one of the porches, an old man sat talking to two or three boys. He was a teacher. He was teaching and disputing and going over points of Moslem observance and belief in the same place where Jesus disputed with a similar "elder" in the cloisters of Herod's Temple. When I turned to the north I saw that the view was blocked by a tall wall and a building.

It is known as the old Turkish Barracks and was so used by the Turks up to the British occupation. This stands on the site of the Castle of Antonia, the Roman stronghold which overlooked Herod's Temple and in which Jesus was charged before Pontius Pilate. The ghost of Antonia frowned down on the ghost of Herod's Temple as it used to do in the days of Christ. In a city where all relics of Roman days are buried thirty, forty, and sixty feet below the debris of the centuries, the Dome of the Rock seems to bring one out into the daylight. It is easier to reconstruct the past in this Moslem sanctuary than it is in the Church of the Holy Sepulcher. It is easy to imagine Jesus preaching in an open space like that of the Temple area, and afterward leaving by one of the gates and going down toward the Mount of Olives on the other side of the wall. The reason why the Temple area is less confusing than other sites in Jerusalem is because it is the only spot that has not been built on again and again: it has descended to us essentially unchanged since the time of Christ. In His day it was a central shrine with a cluster of sacred buildings surrounded by wide paved courts; and that description is still true of it.

I climbed up on a kind of sentry walk on the eastern wall and looked across the Kedron Valley to the Mount of Olives. Not far away in this wall is the blocked-up Golden Gate, standing, it is said, on the site of the gate through which Jesus entered Jerusalem in triumph. Among the numbers of small domed buildings that are grouped about the enclosure is one known as Solomon's Throne. The story—and every inch of the mosque area is embroidered with legend—is that Solomon was found dead on this spot. The Arabs say that he did not wish the demons, over whose kingdom he held authority, to know when he was dead: so, when he realized he was dying, he propped himself up on his throne and sat there as if he were still living, his staff in his hand. And the demons thought that he was alive until the day came when worms gnawed through the staff and the dead body of Solomon crashed to the floor.

The Holy of Holies of the Jewish Temple stood uplifted above the general level of the surrounding courts, and in the same manner the domed shrine of the Rock is today elevated on a platform twelve feet high, which you approach by flights of steps. When I reached the entrance three or four small boys flung themselves on my feet and attempted to tear off my shoes. I have always found it an excellent plan to resist on principal the impetuous ministrations of the Arab until one discovers them to be inevitable. One generally discovers that they are not inevitable. And so it happened at the entrance to the Dome of the Rock. An elderly man in a brown robe approached me, holding two enormous barge-like slippers, worn down at the heels and furnished with long tapes. These he fitted over my shoes, and I shuffled into the Dome of the Rock.

This shrine is unquestionably the most exquisite building in Jerusalem. It is a dim, eight-sided building whose dome is erected on columns of magnificent porphyry, breccia and other tinted stones, all of them picked up by the Moslems from the ruins of Roman Jerusalem. Most of the columns are still fitted with their Byzantine capitals, and a few of them are still marked with the sign of the cross.

An English guide who was taking a few visitors around was explaining the beauty of the windows, and telling his hushed audience that he could go there every day and find some new beauty in the stained glass. I have no doubt he could.

In the center of the exquisite building is something so primitive that you hold your breath. Lying behind an intricate screen of metalwork is a huge, unsmoothed slab of the living rock. It is black in color and polished by time; and it lies there as out of place and as improbable as a ton of coals in the middle of a drawing-room floor. All this finnicky beauty has been built around this huge, sloping slice of Mount Moriah. But the more you think about it, the more improbable it looks, until at last it becomes terrifying. It is as if the sharp top of a mountain were pushing its way through the floor of a house. There is something uncanny and unnatural about it. The rock, as it lies there jutting out about four or six feet above the pavement and streaked with a few bars of red or blue light from the stained-glass windows, seems to take on a powerful and sinister life of its own. One feels that it might move a little in its sleep and shake down the building above it as a sleeping giant might brush away the leaves that have fallen on him.

This is the same rock around which Solomon built his temple, the rock on which the Jewish altar of burnt offerings once stood.

All kinds of thoughts crowd into the mind in this place. But the ideas of another age and of another faith break into one's reverie. The guardian of the shrine shows with great reverence a gold casket in which are preserved two hairs of Mahomet's beard. He tells you that from the black rock the Prophet rose to heaven on the back of his winged steed el-Barûk—"Lightning." And he says that beneath the rock can sometimes be heard an awful sound which is the roaring of all the waters of the flood.

At one side of the rock a flight of eleven steps goes down into a cavern. From this place it is possible to trace a channel cut in the rock which drained the blood of the sacrifices and carried it into the Valley of the Kedron. In this cave there is a flagstone that gives a hollow ring when you strike it. There are all kinds of queer stories about it. What lies underneath no one knows, and I believe that no bribe has ever succeeded in gaining permission for an investigation. One cannot help wondering what lies beneath the Temple area and what marvels the spade might reveal. It is a provoking speculation. It is known that immense rock cisterns exist there, and also the remains of the bathrooms in which priests who suffered ceremonial defilement in Herod's time might wash themselves and leave the Temple secretly. But what else lies hidden there?

Many people believe that if this problem could be investigated something wonderful would be discovered, perhaps the Ark of the Covenant or those vessels of the Temple worship which were not carried to Rome for the triumph of Titus. But the Moslems refuse to allow excavation and so the Temple area remains one of the most tantalizing mysteries in the world.

I left the mosque exhausted by sight-seeing. Nowhere on earth are there in one city two places which so powerfully excite the imagination as the site of Solomon's Temple and the burial place of Jesus Christ.

§ 5

About eighty-five years ago a man named Barclay was walking around the walls of Jerusalem with his dog and a gun. When he came to the Damascus Gate he discovered that the dog was missing. He whistled, but the animal did not appear. Turning back he saw the dog crawling out apparently from beneath the city walls, where he had evidently made a find. He stood barking, asking his master to come and look at his discovery. When Barclay went over, he found that bushes, shrubs, and the debris of centuries concealed the opening to a cavern which ran under the walls and beneath the city.

Such a discovery in Jerusalem fires the imagination and encourages the wildest rumors. The Arabs believe to this day, as I have just said, that in such a cavern the gold and silver treasures of Solomon, the Ark of the Covenant, and the vessels used in the Temple sacrifices, lie waiting to be found. This dream is not confined to the Arabs. I have heard several men, whose opinions claim respect and attention, say that they believe the Ark of the Covenant is hidden somewhere in the mysterious and quite unknown underworld of the Temple area.

So Barclay wisely said nothing and, returning on the following day with a search party, widened the small hole into which his dog had jumped and entered the cavern.

The torches of the search party lit up a weird and terrifying scene. The explorers stood in a snow-white cavern, so large that its extremity was hidden in the darkness. One glance at the stone walls told them that it had been artificially made. The torchlight was not powerful enough to penetrate to the end of the cavern. It was an immense excavation that ran on and on beneath the streets of the Old City.

It was soon realized that they had discovered Solomon's Quarries—called by Josephus the "Royal Quarries"—the quarries which, lost for nearly two centuries, had provided the stone for Solomon's Temple about nine hundred years before Christ.

I think these quarries are one of the most interesting sights in Jerusalem. They are neglected by the average sight-seer, although every Freemason who visits Jerusalem is aware of them. Masons from all parts of the world hold lodge meetings there at night, when they will not be disturbed or observed, because they hold the theory that the builders of the Temple were the first Freemasons.

When I visited the quarries, an old Arab who sits at the entrance gave me a lantern and warned me not to fall down any of the frightful precipices, for Solomon's quarries are no place for the shortsighted or the stumbler.

Another Arab, working in the patch of daylight that penetrates the cave, was shaping paper weights and small hammers such as chairmen use at meetings. These objects, when decorated with appropriate triangles and compasses, are eagerly bought by masonic visitors and find their way all over the world. Stones from the quarries are also exported to become foundation stones for masonic buildings.

I went into the darkness, swinging my lantern, and the path led steeply down into an enormous entrance cave like a buried cathedral. From this excavation wide, high passages led off in many directions. I pulled up sharply on the edge of chasms and, waving my lantern in the darkness, saw that the rock fell away to lower workings, to more distant and deeper caverns.

It has been estimated that in ancient times sufficient stone had been removed from these quarries to build the modern city of Jerusalem twice over. It is a peculiar and unusual pure white stone, soft to work but hardening rapidly when exposed to the atmosphere. The Arabs call these caverns the "cotton caves" because they are so white. Here and there, however, when I flashed my lantern toward the lower portions of the roof, I saw a number of black patches. In one place I was near enough to see that they were large bats, hanging to the roof and waiting for the night.

On every hand I noticed the sign of workmen. With a feeling of awe and bewilderment, a feeling that I was dropping down through the very floor of Time, I knew that these workmen had been dead for nearly three thousand years. Yet the marks made by the Phoenician stonecutters when Solomon was king of Jerusalem were as clean, as sharp and, apparently, as recent, as the marks a man sees in the quarries today.

The workmen had cut niches in the walls for their lamps. And it all seemed so new, so modern, that I had the odd feeling that it was lunch hour during the building of the Temple and that at any moment I might hear the returning feet of Solomon's quarrymen, kicking aside the chips and stones as they poured back to work.

I propped the lantern on a ledge of rock, and by the light of its candle I read the extraordinarily detailed account of the building of the Temple which you will find in the *Second Book of Chronicles,* chapter two, and the *First Book of Kings,* chapter five.

· 43

I suppose a modern architect could not, given the same number of words, create for us a more accurate and vivid picture of the plans, designs, engagement of workmen, rates of pay, building, and furnishing of a great building, than is to be found in these chapters of the Bible.

Down in the darkness of Solomon's Quarries, with the white dust of the stone on my clothes, the building of the Temple took on a reality that surprised me. It frequently happens in Palestine that some verse of the Bible, hitherto meaningless, suddenly unlocks itself, and one is left amazed by its minute accuracy. I realized the real meaning of a verse which must have puzzled many people. Verse seven, in the sixth chapter of the *First Book of Kings,* describing the building of the House of the Lord, says:

"And the house, when it was in building, was built of stone made ready before it was brought thither: so that there was neither hammer nor ax nor any tool of iron heard in the house, while it was in building."

I have always imagined that this verse meant that the Temple stone was quarried far away out of earshot of Jerusalem. What else could it have meant? But why should the writer of *Kings* have stressed the obvious fact that distant quarrying could not be heard on Mount Moriah? Obviously the point of this verse is that the stone with which Solomon built his Temple came almost from beneath the Temple, yet *not a soul heard the cutting of the stones!*

In these quarries you can see how the stone was broken from the bed, how it was passed at once to the masons, who shaped and smoothed it—the floor is in places many feet

44 ·

deep in tons of chips—and how it went straight into the daylight ready to take its place in the building of the Temple.

No matter how earnestly those in the streets of the city above might have listened for the sound of hammers, they could have heard nothing.

Many stories are, of course, told of a mysterious underground passage which linked the quarries with the Temple. There is a widespread belief that the priests hurriedly hid the Temple treasure in these caverns when the Roman armies under Titus razed Jerusalem and the Temple to the ground. I do not know why treasure hunters should still think it possible to find these precious objects, for it is quite clear that many of them were carried through the streets of Rome when Titus celebrated his triumph. However, one earnest explorer some years ago probed for a secret passage —and found one! In order to reach it you have to bend down and crawl for a few yards into a narrow tunnel about three feet in height, and then you find yourself in another passage of the rock. You are at the extremity of the quarries now and moving under Jerusalem in the direction of the Temple Mount. Suddenly you come up against an ancient fortified wall. What it was for, who built it and when it was built, no one knows.

I left the quarries and went out into the blinding light of afternoon with the feeling that yesterday and today are one in the empty caverns where, it seems, the workmen of Hiram, King of Tyre, have just "knocked off" for a ten-minute break.

§ 6

Early one Sabbath morning a young Jew took me around the synagogues in the old city. It was extraordinarily interesting. We plunged straight into the Old Testament. The narrow streets and the labyrinth of houses are full of synagogues, often merely a small room containing a few books on shelves or cupboards, a tribune, and a reading desk on which stood the Torah, or Pentateuch, written on parchment and fixed to rollers.

Ancient Jews, with spectacles on the tips of their noses, rocked themselves backward and forward as they recited prayers; little boys and young men kept up a perpetual swaying and muttering as they repeated the sacred words.

In a synagogue of Moroccan Jews the congregation sat on the floor like Moors and the women were hidden, like wives in a harem, behind an openwork screen.

In nearly all these synagogues I saw something that illuminated a passage in *St. Luke:* the story of Jesus as a child of twelve disputing with the rabbis in the Temple. There were small boys in their Sabbath clothes, prayer-rugs over their shoulders, sitting beside their fathers or their grandfathers, and carefully applying themselves to the Law, repeating the words in monotonous voices and rocking their small bodies.

In one obscure synagogue, I think of Ashkenazim Jews, the morning service had just ended. A lad of about twelve years of age was standing before three bearded elders, talking to them in a precocious and animated manner. Sometimes he pleased them, and they smiled and patted him on the shoulder; but sometimes he annoyed them, and the

46 .

three old men shook their beards in disagreement and
frowned at the lad over their spectacles. But the little fellow stood his ground, waiting respectfully to be spoken to;
then, his questions over, he gave a little bob to the old men
and walked slowly away.

This, I thought, must have been something like the sight
that met the eyes of Joseph and Mary when, seeking Jesus,
"they found Him in the Temple, sitting in the midst of the
doctors, both hearing them and asking them questions."

We came to a door in a high wall. A woman peered out
through a little grid, but refused to open the door. The
young Jew begged to be admitted, but she was adamant.
This was the carefully guarded underground synagogue of
the Qaarites, whose community was once numerous.
These Jews have a peculiar story.

In 1762 the Turkish government demanded a huge sum
of money from the Jews and, in order to discuss the demand
in secret, the Chief Rabbi ordered a meeting in the synagogue of the Qaarites. On the way down the Chief Rabbi
felt ill and stumbled. Some of his followers, suspecting
black magic, began to tear up the stairs, and found copies
of the works of the Rabbi Moses Ben Maimon, which the
Qaarites had buried so that they could show their contempt by walking over them. The horrified Chief Rabbi
then and there pronounced a curse on the sacrilegious
Qaarite community. The curse was that they would never
be able to form the quorum of ten grown males necessary
for public worship.

"They still live under the curse," said the young Jew.
"About a hundred years ago there was great joy among
them when several Qaarite families came to Jerusalem

· 47

from the Crimea. At last, they thought, they would be able to worship together. But the emigrants caught the plague. Some of the men died in the streets of Jerusalem and the others died when they reached their lodgings. Today there are only five or six Qaarite men left, so that the Chief Rabbi's curse is still on them and they can never bring a 'Minyan' together. . . ."

While he was talking, the grid in the door was softly withdrawn and an old, very dark, very sad eye gazed out at us. Then the gird was softly shut. The young Jew knocked again. But there was no answer.

§ 7

I am sure that Hezekiah's Tunnel will never become a popular sight with visitors to Palestine. It is wet, messy and dangerous, and you have to explore it at night in order not to stir up the water of the Virgin's Fountain in which the women of Siloam wash their clothes during the daytime.

I was determined to explore this tunnel, but I could find no one in Jerusalem who had been through it or who would offer to go through it with me. One man said that he would take me to the Siloam end of the tunnel and then go over to the Virgin's Fountain and wait for my body; but I did not like the idea of going through it alone.

Eventually I encountered a member of the American Colony who has explored most places around Jerusalem, and he agreed to accompany me.

So one night, just before moonrise, we went down to the Zion Gate and took those dark, mysterious roads that lie beyond the walls of Jerusalem and lead steeply down into

the Valley of Hinnom, which is Ge Hinnom or Gehenna—
otherwise hell. It was in this valley that the abominable
rites of Baal were observed, and somewhere in it once stood
the fires of Moloch in which children were sacrificed.

We went down into a stony wilderness bleached white by
the thousands of gravestones which rise on both slopes of
the valley, marking the graves of Jews and Moslems who
wish to be first on the Resurrection morning. A few lights
on a hill marked the squalid little village of Siloam. Somewhere in the darkness to our right was the Field of Blood,
which the Chief Priests bought with the silver of Judas.

We had to pick our way carefully, flashing electric torches
on the stony track. Behind us came an Arab carrying lanterns and thigh boots.

While we stumbled downward in single file, sometimes
straying from the path and tripping over stones, I thought
how astonishing it is that, while so much of old Jerusalem
has perished, this tunnel of Hezekiah, one of its earliest relics, should exist today almost as it was seven hundred years
before Christ.

Hezekiah was king in Jerusalem when the Assyrian was
preparing to come down "like a wolf on the fold." If you
wish to feel the terror that seized Jerusalem at a time when
men lived in fear of hearing the Assyrian battering-rams
against the walls, read the denunciatory thunder of Isaiah.
He lived through this dangerous reign, and his writings re-
buke Jerusalem for her sins and promise God's vengeance
on the enemy.

King Hezekiah, forced to contemplate a siege, was troubled by the fact that the only spring of water in these bar-

ren hills—now called the Virgin's Fountain—lay just outside the walls of the old City of David.

Jerusalem could not exist long if her water supply fell into the hands of the Assyrians. So, by cutting a long underground tunnel, the king brought the spring water into the city. He then decided to seal up the spring and hide it from the advancing army of Sennacherib, so that the Assyrians would not be able to cut off Jerusalem's water supply. This scheme, which must have been carried out in frantic haste, is mentioned three times in the Bible: in *Second Chronicles, Second Kings,* and *Isaiah.* In *Chronicles* it is recorded:

> "And when Hezekiah saw that Sennacherib was come, and that he was purposed to fight against Jerusalem, he took counsel with his princes and his mighty men to stop the waters of the fountains which were without the city: and they did help him. So there was gathered much people together; who stopped all the fountains, and the brook that ran through the midst of the land, saying, 'Why should the kings of Assyria come, and find much water?' "

The historical accuracy of these verses was not realized until, some years ago, two boys playing in the valley discovered the tunnel and managed to crawl through it.

My American friend and I came down to the Pool of Siloam, where we put on our waders by the light of a torch held by the Arab. The tunnel was a black hole in the side of the hill, from which water about two feet in depth was flowing. There was a weird echo in it, as if people were whispering in the darkness.

50 .

"There's nobody there," said my friend. "No Arab would go through the tunnel at night. We are hearing echoes from a mosque on the hill."

As we waded into the tunnel our electric torches lit up the flow of brownish water and the clammy walls. The cutting was perhaps fourteen feet high and only two feet wide, but the height was never the same for very long. The marks made by the axes of the workmen of King Hezekiah were sharp and clear on the stone.

The first three hundred feet were simple, but then the tunnel became low and we had to walk bent double. There were also potholes in which we suddenly sank well over the knees. The total length of the tunnel is over a quarter of a mile, so that I had plenty of time to regret my decision to explore it and to admire the common sense of all those people who refused to go with me!

What a weird experience it was, this slow splash through a tunnel which Isaiah must have seen in the making, a tunnel cut seven hundred years before the birth of Christ in the shadow of a hill on which Solomon's Temple was still standing.

It was clear that the tunnel had been made by two parties of men working toward each other from both ends. They worked in great haste and paid no attention to uniformity of workmanship. The main factor was time and the only thing that mattered was to bring the water within the walls of Jerusalem as quickly as possible.

I was interested to see that, here and there, the working parties had apparently lost their sense of direction. The tunnel would go in the wrong direction for a foot or so, and then, as if the men had stopped to listen for the picks of the other party working toward them, resume in the right direction. In the center we came to the place where the two parties met.

A mystery about Hezekiah's Tunnel which no one has yet solved is why, at a time when every moment was precious, did the workmen cut a winding tunnel 1,749 feet in length, when the direct measurement from the two points is only 1,098 feet? Why should they have cut through an unnecessary 651 feet of rock?

A once popular explanation was that they bent the tunnel to avoid the rock tombs of David and Solomon. This theory has fired the imagination of archaeologists and treasure hunters and has led several men to dig for these tombs; but nothing has ever been discovered.

As we splashed onward the roof of the tunnel became higher and the water cleaner. I knew that we were coming out toward the Virgin's Fountain. Suddenly we heard the sound of running water and, wading through a large rock pool, waist-high in parts, we came out into a clear, moonlit night. We were at the bottom of the flight of steps that goes down to the Virgin's Fountain. There we peeled off our waders and put on our shoes.

We climbed out into the Kedron Valley. I looked up and saw, high above me to the left, the walls of Jerusalem with the moonlight over them. As we went on through the lonely valley with its crowded tombs, we came to the foot of the Mount of Olives and saw the little walled Garden of Gethsemane, with the light of the moon falling between its cypress trees and lying across its quiet paths.

CHAPTER TWO

I go down to Jericho and visit the Inn of the Good Samaritan. I find Jericho in a trench of tropical heat and I explore the shores of the Dead Sea and come to the river Jordan.

§ 1

One of the most exciting things to do in Jerusalem is to take a car and run down to the Dead Sea, the Jordan and Jericho.

There is perhaps no contrast anywhere more remarkable than that of Jerusalem mounted 2,300 feet *above* the sea and the Jordan Valley, only twenty-three miles away but 1,300 feet *below* sea level. Just think what this means in climate and temperature. In less than an hour you leave a city swept by fresh mountain winds and you plunge down into tropical heat where bananas and sugar cane are growing and where the stagnant waters of the Dead Sea accumulate a white crust of chemicals.

When I told a friend that I intended to "run down" to the Dead Sea for a day, he said:

"Well, be careful to get back before dark."

"Why?" I asked.

"You might meet Abu Jildah . . ."

"Who is Abu Jildah?"

"He is a brigand who has shot several policemen. There is a price on his head, and he has a habit of building a wall of stones across the Jericho road, stopping cars, robbing you, and, if you resist, shooting you. He once held up fourteen cars in a row on this road, robbed everyone, threatened to cut off a woman's finger because her rings were tight, and was off and away to the hills by the time the police heard about it. So take my tip and get back before dusk. . . ."

As my friend was giving me this advice I remembered the Parable of the Good Samaritan: "a certain man went down from Jerusalem to Jericho, and fell among thieves, who stripped him of his raiment, and wounded him, and departed, leaving him half dead."

"Do you think," I asked, "that the man who fell among thieves was attacked by someone like Abu Jildah?"

"There is no doubt about it," my friend replied. "The road from Jerusalem to Jericho has been notorious throughout history for its robberies. It is, as you will see, perfect brigand country. It has been suggested that Jesus, in the Parable of the Good Samaritan, was weaving a parable around an actual hold-up. He told the story on His way up from Jericho to Bethany on the Mount of Olives, which rather supports this theory. Halfway down to Jericho you will see an old khan, or inn, on the side of the road—in fact it is the only building, apart from a police post, that you will meet after Bethany. This is believed to be the inn mentioned by Jesus in the parable. No doubt it is so, because its rock cisterns prove that an inn has stood on this spot since Bible times. You should stop and go inside. . . . But don't forget to be back before dark!"

I set off at ten o'clock. I passed the Damascus Gate and drove along the road through the Kedron Valley. It runs to the left, and around this corner Jerusalem was hidden from view. My attention became fixed on a downward road and a succession of nasty corners.

About three miles from Jerusalem a superb panorama of the Dead Sea country lay before me. I could see the white road twisting and turning into a sterile wilderness of parched rock, dropping ever downward into bleakness and solitude. I stopped the car and got out.

I thought that I had never seen anything that looked more like the primitive conception of hell. It was the sort of place that an early Italian painter would have peopled with hairy little devils with horns and forked tails. The hillsides were either littered with millions of limestone chips or else they were bare and volcanic. Some of the hills were domed or cone-shaped like young volcanoes and others were queerly twisted, tortured and deformed as if chewed up by fire like the clinkers that come out of a furnace.

While I was looking at the terrifying panorama of the Dead Sea, a plump and smiling Arab came up to me holding several slings. He selected a pebble and, whirling the sling around his head, suddenly shot the stone into the air. I watched it drop into a valley half a mile below. He then pointed to a sling and to me, suggesting that I should buy one. To my astonishment I did buy one! Why, I shall never know.

§ 2

The heat became insufferable and the wilderness seemed to close in on me as I continued my journey. The air was hot and still. The khaki rocks flung back the sun like the sides of a furnace. Soon there was but little green to be seen. Black goats were grazing on tufts of coarse grass which grew in the cracks of the rock. Turning a corner, I almost ran into a herd of them. They scattered and leaping to the rocks, their long ears flapping, turned to watch me go by like angry, bearded old men.

Once I met a shepherd painfully climbing the hill, leading his sheep, talking to them all the time, and on his shoulder he carried a lamb, holding it by the four legs as in pictures of the Good Shepherd.

The road now had a sharp cliff on one side and on the other a drop into a ravine. It was never straight for very long.

I ran downward to the first sign of life, a well—known as the Fountain of the Apostles, from which an old man was filling a pitcher. On my right, a narrow footpath ran back through the hills to Jerusalem. This was the ancient short cut to Bethany, and the road that Jesus and His Disciples would have taken when they went up to the Passover and the Last Supper.

It was not difficult to understand why this road has always been the haunt of bandits. It is a road whose serpentine bends and overhanging cliffs might have been designed for highway robbery. At hundreds of points are stretches lying between two acute corners and backed by towering cliffs and projecting boulders, where two or three armed men could hold up anything that came along. The robbery once committed, nothing could be easier than an escape into the trackless wilderness, where thousands of caves offer secure hiding places and where a search party might wander without success forever.

The road, after diving steadily downward, began to rise. On the crest of the ridge stood the Inn of the Good Samaritan, called by the Arabs Khan Hathrur. As I stopped outside it a man with three laden donkeys came up and halted them in the shadow of the inn.

The building is the usual Turkish khan made to provide safety for men and beasts during the night, and generally placed within an easy journey of a city. The foundations of the khan, and the ancient rock cisterns below it in which water is stored, prove that an inn has been on this site from Roman times and possibly even earlier. There can be little doubt that this is the inn our Lord was thinking of when He told the Parable of the Good Samaritan, because there has never been any other inn between Jerusalem and Jericho.

The building is an oblong one-story house of uncertain date, entered by a high arched door placed in the center. A large courtyard surrounded by a wall occupies a space of level ground at the back. In the middle of this courtyard is a well from which water is drawn by letting down a bucket on a rope.

I read the Parable of the Good Samaritan as I sat in the shadow of the wall. It is a parable that has gone around the world, but I wonder how many people really understand why Jesus told it. He had said farewell to Galilee and was journeying toward Jerusalem and His Crucifixion. His custom was to visit the synagogues, to preach and afterward to invite discussion. It was probably at Jericho that, after He had preached, a lawyer in the congregation, anxious to display his learning and attempting to provoke Jesus, asked: "Master, what shall I do to inherit eternal life?" The questioner was a dialectician whose business it was to interpret the Jewish Law. His question was obviously a trap, as Jesus realized, for He countered with the question: "What is

written in the Law? How readest thou?", which, turning
the question back on the questioner, meant: "You are a
lawyer. You have studied these things. Let us have your
expert opinion."

The man replied, quoting *Deuteronomy* and *Leviticus,* as
Jesus knew he must: "Thou shalt love the Lord thy God
with all thy heart, and with all thy soul, and with all thy
strength, and with all thy mind; and thy neighbor as thy-
self."

"Thou hast answered right," said Jesus, capping the other's quotation with a paraphrase from *Leviticus:* "this do
and thou shalt live."

But the lawyer, furious at being so swiftly worsted,
thought he still saw a chance to win the battle of wits, and
asked at once: "And who is my neighbor?" It was a new
argument! A Jew's neighbor, according to rabbinical law,
was only a fellow Israelite. No gentile was his neighbor.
The lawyer felt fairly confident that Jesus would depart
from this narrow limitation and would lay Himself open
to a charge of heresy. Jesus, seeing this trap as clearly as
He had seen the other, replied with a parable. He said:

> "A certain man went down from Jerusalem to Jeri-
> cho, and fell among thieves, which stripped him of his
> raiment, and wounded him, and departed, leaving
> him half dead. And by chance there came down a cer-
> tain priest that way: and when he saw him, he passed
> by on the other side. And likewise a Levite, when he
> was at the place, came and looked on him, and passed
> by on the other side. But a certain Samaritan, as he
> journeyed, came where he was: and when he saw him,
> he had compassion on him, and went to him, and

bound up his wounds, pouring in oil and wine, and set him on his own beast, and brought him to an inn, and took care of him. And on the morrow when he departed, he took out two pence, and gave them to the host, and said unto him, Take care of him; and whatsoever thou spendest more, when I come again, I will repay thee."

One can imagine the lawyer writhing unhappily in his seat. He had been trapped as neatly as he had hoped to trap Jesus! He was being forced to admit that one of the loathed race of Samaritans, one of the detested people with whom the Jews had no dealings, was his "neighbor." And the relentless question was put:

"Which now of these three, thinkest thou, was neighbor unto him that fell among the thieves?"

We can sense the lawyer's discomfiture in his reply. He cannot bring himself to utter the detested word, Samaritan. It would stick in his throat. Instead he has to admit:

"He that showed mercy on him."

"Go, and do thou likewise," said Jesus.

Thus a masterpiece of dialectics is concluded with a story, apparently so simple, but floating like a leaf on deeper currents.

§ 3

When I left the Inn of the Good Samaritan I plunged down into a land of fire. There was no shade anywhere. The sun beat in my eyes and quivered over the barren earth. In a little over half an hour I had left a temperate climate for the heat of the tropics.

Coming to a convenient place, I stopped the car and removed my coat, for I was suffocating. I looked into the abyss, where far below, cut in the side of a sand-colored mountain, was a monastery built like a swallow's nest on the wall of a house. The cliffs around about this monastery were pitted with caves in which hermits still live, mortifying the flesh as they did in the Thebaid.

Onward I went down the blinding white road. There was a post with "Sea Level" printed on it; and the road still plunged downward, the heat growing even fiercer. A lizard streaked across the path leaving a twisted trail in the fine white dust. A movement on a hill revealed a group of camels, queer prehistoric-looking creatures the very color of the sandy rocks, grazing with their calves upon the spiky bushes and the unwholesome-looking thorns. Turning a corner, I saw below me a view of the Jordan Valley and of Jericho among its trees and, to the right, the sparkling blue waters of the Dead Sea with the Mountains of Moab, streaked and slashed with shadows, rising from its eastern shores.

Some writers have described this hot gash in the earth's crust as the most horrible place in the world, while others have found it strangely beautiful. It is, I suppose, a matter of temperament or, perhaps, liver. If you are not feeling too well, I can imagine that the Jordan Valley with its overwhelming heat and its airlessness, and Jericho with its flamboyant vegetation, its reptiles and its insects, could be a terrible nightmare. Here, strangely enough, is the same awful sterility which is encountered only on the summit of great mountains. Just as a man venturing alone above the vegetation belt on a high mountain is sometimes seized with a chill of terror, feeling that he is trespassing in the workshop of God, so in this uncanny trench he feels that he is walking where no man was meant to walk. All around are piled dead rocks twisted in the agony of some prehistoric convulsion, unlike the good clean rocks from which men can build their homes: obscene rocks stained with yellow slime and covered with a ghastly shroud of salt.

The plain over which I was looking is about fourteen miles wide at Jericho. On one side of it rise the terrific mountains of Judea and, fourteen miles away, facing them, are the mountains of Moab. The Jordan Valley is a trench between them: a parched wilderness of brown hills that lies sweltering in the burning sunlight, and streaked around the Dead Sea with patches of unhealthy white and dirty gray. In the center meanders a serpentine streak of green. It is formed by the tamarisks, the willows and the green bushes that follow the Jordan's two-hundred-mile windings from the Sea of Galilee, which is, as the crow flies, only sixty-five miles away. And this strange dead-looking world of sandy rock, twisted into weird shapes by ancient disturbances of the earth and stained and streaked with chemicals, is as far below the sea as many a British coal mine.

"There may be something on the surface of another planet to match the Jordan Valley: there is nothing on this," wrote George Adam Smith in his great book *The Historical Geography of the Holy Land.* "No other part of the earth, uncovered with water, sinks to 300 feet below the level of the ocean. But here we have a rift more than one hundred and sixty miles long, and from two to fifteen broad, which falls from the sea level to as deep as 1,292 feet below it at the coast of the Dead Sea, while the bottom of the latter is 1,300 deeper still.

In this trench there are the Jordan, a river nearly one hundred miles long; two great lakes, respectively twelve and fifty-two miles in length; large tracts of arable country, especially about Genesaret, Bethshan and Jericho, regions which were once very populous, like the coasts of the Lake of Galilee; and the sites of some famous towns—Tiberias, Jericho, and 'Cities of the Plain.' Is it not true that on the earth there is nothing else like this deep, this colossal ditch?"

The greenness of Jericho rose up, an oasis in the dreadful desolation. From the height of the road it looked much nearer to the Dead Sea than it actually is, but I was soon to learn that nothing in the strange air of the Jordan Valley is more deceptive than one's idea of distance.

§ 4

Modern Jericho is a hot and dusty collection of mud huts, Arab houses and banana groves. It was fast asleep in the noonday sun. A herd of black goats stood in the dust, and a group of camels sat in the full blaze of the sun protruding their lips and glancing down their noses with an expression of superiority seen at its best elsewhere in the animal kingdom perhaps only on the face of a disapproving aunt.

The Arabs explain the superior expression of the camel in this way. God, they say, has a hundred names but man knows only ninety-nine of them. The camel knows them all!

About two miles from modern Jericho upon a level plain I came upon the ruins of the Old Testament Jericho which fell down, says the Bible, at the blast of a trumpet.

There is nothing today but a huge mound of sun-caked earth and stone from which with the point of a stick you can turn up fragments of ancient pottery. This mound rises to a height of about twenty or thirty feet and from the top you get a good idea of the ruins of houses and the line, here and there, of a narrow, twisting street. The town was evidently a small one, covering about ten acres, and surrounded by a wall perhaps twenty-six feet high and seven feet thick, made of mud bricks on a foundation of stone.

When Moses looked down upon the Promised Land from the heights of Mount Nebo beyond the Dead Sea, he saw this walled town standing in an enormous palm grove surrounded by its gardens. It must have looked to the hungry Israelites the very symbol of luxury and richness. Jericho has been called the "key" and the "guardhouse" of Judea, but George Adam Smith preferred to call it the pantry! It was the first city in the path of the invading Israelites when, after crossing the Jordan under Joshua's leadership, they carried out their famous maneuver with the rams' horns and the Ark of the Covenant.

The excavations which Professor Garstang conducted recently on the site of ancient Jericho seem to prove two very interesting things: that the Biblical computation of the date of the Exodus is more accurate than that of modern Egyptologists, and that the walls of Jericho actually did fall down. It is considered that they were destroyed by an earthquake, or some similar disturbance, which overthrew them with great violence. Wandering over the ruins, I came on a section of the wall that bore obvious traces of this.

After Joshua's destruction of Jericho it seems to have remained a ruin for several centuries. In time another city

. 63

grew up there, a city rich in the vegetation which springs up wherever water is poured on the Jordan Valley, a city of dates and balsam and corn and fruit. Then in the time of Herod the Great it was rebuilt not upon the old site but a few miles away overlooking the Dead Sea. This was the Jericho of the New Testament, the Jericho that Jesus saw. We may imagine a beautiful little town laid out in the Roman manner with dignified colonnades and buildings with classical porticoes. There Herod built his winter palace where, no matter how biting were the winds around Jerusalem, he could enjoy warmth and sunshine; and it was in this palace that, eaten by disease, broken-hearted and remorseful, he died.

I found the remains of this once royal city and it was difficult to believe that men had ever lived there. There was nothing but a number of mounds and hummocks in which I suppose it might have been possible to find an ancient coin or a broken pot. And I tried hard to imagine what it looked like when Jesus saw it as "he went on before, going up to Jerusalem."

§ 5

I dipped my hand in the Dead Sea and held my wet fingers in the sun. In a few seconds a fine white powder formed on my hand which I found bitter and salt to the taste.

The Dead Sea is beautiful to look at on a sunny day. The report spread by medieval pilgrims of its gloom is entirely false and reflects, perhaps, not the Dead Sea but the minds of those gallant voyagers. The story that no birds can fly across it because of poison in the air is also untrue. There

The road that climbs to Nazareth where Jesus spent his boyhood.

The road to Jericho, the probable setting of the Good Samaritan parable.

A monk in the present-day Garden of Gethsemane.

The Sea of Galilee which Jesus knew and loved.

are not many birds because there are no fish in the sea. The few Jordan fish that do get carried into the salt lake are soon cast up mummified on the shores. But the Dead Sea itself is blue and sparkling.

The waters lap the beach of pebbles in oily little waves. There are no shells on the beach, no evidence of any life, no growth of weeds or water plants, for the waters are sterile and dead. The reason why the Dead Sea is a huge cauldron of chemicals is that there is no outlet. It is a vast hole in the earth into which the Jordan and tributary streams pour every day nearly seven million tons of water mixed with sulphurous and nitrous matter. Unable to escape, and subjected to the tremendous heat of the Jordan Valley, this water evaporates, leaving behind enormous deposits of salts and other chemicals in the sea. In the sea bed there are also hot springs about which little is known. Ordinary sea water holds from four to six per cent of solids in solution; Dead Sea water holds five times as much. It is impossible for a bather to sink in it and a nonswimmer out of his depth cannot drown as long as he keeps his head. When Titus came to the Jordan Valley in 70 A.D. he caused several slaves to be chained together and flung into the Dead Sea. But they evidently kept their heads, for they emerged alive.

Any horror inspired by the Dead Sea is due to its appalling setting: the dreadful banks of chemical slime, the gray landslides of salt, the smell of sulphur, the weird, twisted foothills stained and tortured like the deposit at the bottom of a crucible. The hills are not shaped like ordinary hills: they are more like the fantastic outlines of cooled metal. As one wanders along the desolate shores the fate of Sodom and Gomorrah, which one may, possibly, have thought of as a tragic allegory, becomes terrifyingly real. It is as though this frightful judgment on human sin has forever blasted and unhallowed the shores of the Dead Sea.

It was believed at one time that the ruins of those cities lie below the salt waters, but I understand that archaeologists are looking for them around the shores. It is all part of the macabre setting that a mountain of salt, which the Arabs have mined for centuries, should exist far to the south, a strange place where twisted white pillars were recognized by the Jews in the time of Josephus as the remains of Lot's wife.

"Then the Lord rained upon Sodom and Gomorrah brimstone and fire. . . ."

The words of *Genesis* take on a horrible significance as one explores the Dead Sea. Fire has smitten the land, piled up the hills in tangled confusion and ripped great rents in the earth's body; and even today the smell of brimstone has not faded from the land.

§ 6

The river Jordan flows south from Galilee and empties itself into the Dead Sea. You can follow its course by a double line of tamarisks and willows growing upon its banks.

I took a road straight across the hills toward what is known as the place of Christ's baptism. It was not really a road: it was an ill-defined cart track that lost itself in thorn bushes, found itself again in holes and swamps and went on twisting and winding toward the thin belt of green that marks the course of the Jordan.

No one knows where the place of the Baptism was, neither do we know where "Bethany beyond Jordan" was. But the place I discovered among the tamarisks and the willows is that which has been hallowed by centuries of pious pilgrimage. In the old days before Communism, when Russia was "Holy Russia," thousands of pilgrims used to come down to this place to plunge into the Jordan, wearing white gowns which they took home to keep as their shrouds. To-day there are few pilgrims. The custom of bathing at this spot, or somewhere near it, goes back to the most remote times. It was known to the Pilgrim of Bordeaux, who visited the Holy Land in the Roman era—about the year 333 A.D., and one evening in the year 1172 Theodoric saw sixty thousand persons plunge into the river at this spot.

I was not prepared for the strange sight at the end of the road. On the river bank is an odd café, or rest house, mounted on stilts. The roof is made of Jordan reeds, and everything about it suggests that any moment the narrow, inoffensive river might overflow and drive the few inhabitants to their boats. Under this frail shelter are set a number of homemade tables and chairs. Hens, chickens, turkeys and goats roam carelessly around the tables. A stuffed crane and a stuffed flamingo, both much the worse for wear, hang with dreary reluctance from the roof. There is a kind of counter, or bar, with a notice which states that this collection of poles and reeds is owned by Mr. N. Stomation. I discovered that the only visible inhabitant was someone, whom I took to be Mr. Stomation, sitting with his back to the Jordan gloomily whittling a stick with a penknife. He was in his shirt sleeves, with an ancient khaki tunic flung across his shoulders. He paid no attention to me as I prowled about his strange retreat. The Jordan is apparently always trying to dislodge Mr. Stomation. His dwelling quarters, and also a large dome-shaped oven, are mounted on twelve-foot-high stilts. Even the chickens and the turkeys and the goats must sometimes be forced to run for it, as little pile dwellings to the side of the main quarters testify

The Jordan, flowing a few yards from this tattered, pre-historic-looking encampment, surprised me. I felt that I was standing on the bank of some English stream, perhaps the Avon in Warwickshire high up beyond the mill in flood time. I cannot say why I should have felt this, because the banks of the Jordan are thick with exotic, foreign trees and shrubs such as tamarisk and a thin reed, like bamboo. I think it was the way a group of willows dropped their leaves in the water exactly as they do when the Avon floods the meadows around Stratford-on-Avon in March. And as I looked at the Jordan touching the willow leaves and moving them the way of the current, I seemed to be back again in the great happiness of my youth, sitting upon an old green wall near Holy Trinity. There is something slow and gentle and small about the Jordan as it swings around the bend beside the place of the Baptism; something, as I say, very homelike that made me think of those devout paintings on the walls of Venice and Florence in which men have painted Bethlehem and Nazareth like their own towns. It seemed to me that there should be a lesson in this, but a better moralist than myself would have to make it: that a man should travel across the world to see the holy Jordan, and discover it to be just like the little stream at home that runs at the bottom of his garden.

I thought how true this vision of mine was, and how it would probably be contradicted by every tourist who has seen the milky-blue and sandy whirlpools of this river. For the Jordan does flow in every part of the Christian world. Some little drop finds its way into every font at every baptism.

On the way back I came to a deserted place near the river where a new church was standing among trees. It was the only building in the wilderness. While I was looking at it, a black monk came out of a side door and stood watching me; and I remembered that someone had told me the Abyssinians had dedicated a church to St. John not far from the river. Before the church was built, the monks used to live in odd little dwellings perched in the trees, more or less like Mr. Stomation's restaurant.

I went up and, by signs made the monk understand that I would like to see the church. He beamed with pleasure and his teeth shone like snow in the night of his countenance. Leading the way, he unlocked a door and took me into a beautifully designed church, the high altar hidden, as is the custom with the Abyssinians, behind closed doors, and a great space all around the church for the processions which are a great feature of the mysterious African devo-

. 69

tions. He took me into the vestry and showed with great pride a series of brilliant vestments, reds and blues and purples, some of them roughly sewn with bits of tinsel and gold braid. We never spoke a word, but we made many signs, smiled, nodded and bowed. When I went, anxious to give something to the church, for the Abyssinians are very poor, I brought out some silver, but a look of pain shot into the eyes of the monk and he gently pushed away my hand and shook his head. His eyes were like those of some big, gentle animal.

There is something very touching about these black men who worship Christ with such primitive but, I am told, heretical devotion. I have never encountered any people who seem so gentle and so meek.

§ 7

I got back to Jericho as the afternoon sun was sinking and left my car. I was anxious to be on the mountain road before dark, but I was also determined to climb the Mount of Temptation which rises at the back of Jericho.

It was a long but easy ascent, and with every step upward the Jordan Valley looked more terrible in its hot bleached bareness. When I reached the top of this mountain I was still two hundred feet below sea level.

Halfway up, built partly in the rock, I discovered a monastery where ten old Greek monks endure the poverty that has descended on the Eastern Church. Few pilgrims come now to pray in the little grotto where Jesus fasted in the wilderness.

70 ·

One old man, who could speak two or three words of English, took me over the chapel, with its dust, its dim, gaudy ikons, its unlit candles, and its air of decay and neglect.

He pointed to a cavity beneath an altar, telling me in a solemn low voice that it was the cave in which Jesus slept before He was tempted by the devil. Then he tiptoed off to some other dusty shrine. The air of death about the place, and the old men who tottered about in their black robes, were rather depressing. Then the setting was so improbable and fantastic. A monastery carved out of a mountainside, bits of it built out here and there over ghastly chasms, while other parts of it were cut into the face of the mountain so that the walls and roof were of the rock. I wondered what happened when one of these old men died. I imagined them cutting a grave in the rock and placing their companion to rest like some ancient Moses on Nebo.

There was something pathetic in their childish pleasure in my visit. The old monk, having shown me the church, led me to a room whose balcony was built out over a sheer drop of more than a thousand feet. The little wooden erection shook so ominously under me that I stepped back into the room. It was a strange little room, furnished according to some dimly remembered standards of the distant earth. A little table with a green cloth occupied the center, and around the walls were set old horsehair padded chairs. The only pictures in the room were of the Tzar and the Tzarina, King Tino of Greece and, strangely enough, old-fashioned colored lithographs of King George V and Queen Mary of Britain.

The old monk sat with folded hands, smiling affably at me and speaking the most atrocious English.

"Ah!" he said, or rather meant to say, glancing up at the lithograph of the Tzar, "poor, poor Russia!"

He told me that in the old days the mountain path was black with ascending pilgrims from Holy Russia. But now . . . he spread his hands in a gesture of despair. At this point a young monk, the only young one I had seen, entered bearing a tray containing small cups of coffee, little plates of jam and a white liqueur that tasted like absinthe. I drank the coffee and the liqueur and ate the jam, ceremoniously bowing to the old monk from time to time and receiving in return his smiles and bows. The young monk, a rather scared-looking youth in spectacles and with side-whiskers of brown fluff, stood holding the tray and bowing stiffly every time I put back a glass or a plate.

It was the habit in ancient times to treat any stranger as if he might be a wandering Christ, and this beautiful courtesy still exists in out-of-the-way parts of the earth. We have lost it, and with it something fine and beautiful has gone from our lives. When the old monk led me to the main gate and, lifting the latch for me, said good-by, adding a blessing in Greek, his eyes still held that antique wonder in them. I was a stranger going down and away into mystery. I turned and waved back to him, and went on down the stony path.

Never shall I forget the sunset flung back upon the hills of Moab, turning them to pink and mauve, filling the gashes in their flanks with blue shadows. The brown humped hills lay to the north like a map of the moon, and in the center

The Church of the Nativity in Bethlehem, built above a cave long recognized as the birthplace of Jesus.

The Jordan River, near where Jesus is believed to have been baptized.

Fishermen mending their precious nets.

of the wilderness I saw the green thread that marks the river whose waters flow to the four corners of Christendom.

There were shadows over the mountain pass as I went up to Jerusalem. The sun had gone when I passed Bethany. In Jerusalem they were lighting the lamps.

CHAPTER THREE

In Bethlehem I enter the Grotto of the Nativity and meet the descendants of the Crusaders. I travel to Beersheba, where I attend a sitting of a tribal court. I watch camels bathing in the sea at Ascalon and, in the country round about, I notice many Biblical scenes and characters.

§ 1

Bethlehem is only five miles away from Jerusalem and I thought it would be interesting to walk there. As I set off early one morning I reflected how short are the distances in the Holy Land. When the Bible says that Moses was shown the Promised Land from Mount Nebo it is literally true. From the height of four thousand feet above the Dead Sea he would see the entire country.

As I walked on, I thought that travel in Palestine is different from travel in any other part of the world because Palestine exists already in our imagination before we start out. From our earliest years it begins to form in our minds side by side with fairyland, so that it is often difficult to tell where one begins and the other ends. Therefore the Palestine of reality is always in conflict with the imaginary Palestine, so violently at times that many people cannot give up this imaginary Palestine without a feeling of loss. That is why some people go away disillusioned from the Holy Land. They are unable, or unwilling, to reconcile the real with the ideal.

Any truthful account of travel in Palestine must mention

this conflict. Every day you hear travelers say, as they visit some place: "I never imagined it quite like that," or "I always thought of it in a different way."

And as I went on to Bethlehem I remembered a place hushed in snow where shepherds wrapped in thick cloaks watched their flocks under the frosty stars. There was a little shelter in this place in which beasts stamped in their stalls and blew the fog of their breath into the cold air. On the straw near the mangers, sitting in exquisite detachment, was a Mother with a gold circle about her head and a little Child. The stars shone coldly, and through the air came a sound of far-off bells.

I know perfectly well that this picture was edged with gilt. It was my own private little vision of Bethlehem, something that has been with me all my life, something made up in my mind from Christmas cards sent to me when I was a child, from pictures that I loved before I could read, something formed by the piety and reverence which a cold northern land has cast around the story of the Nativity. Every Christian nation has translated the story of Christ into its own idiom and cradled Him in its own barns.

I had only to feel the airless heat and to glance at the white dust of the road, the plodding camels, the patient donkeys, the Arabs squatting in the shade of walls, to know that Bethlehem was not going to look like a Christmas card; and in some queer way I felt sorry.

I came to a place where a few trees made a pool of shade on the dust of the road. And under the trees was an old well with a stone basin beside it, so that shepherds and camelmen could pour out water for their beasts.

This well, like so many things in this land, has several

names. Some call it Mary's Well, because of an old story that the Holy Family, traveling the five miles between Bethlehem and Jerusalem, once rested there and drank its waters. It is also called the Well of the Star. The legend is that the Wise Men on their way to Bethlehem lost the Star and, coming to this well to slake their thirst, found it again shining in the water.

I went on past the Well of the Star. On the left the earth suddenly fell into space. The terrific landslide fell away into the heat, and down below, far off, like land seen from an airplane, lay a brown-and-blue map of the Dead Sea and the Mountains of Moab. Ahead of me was Bethlehem, with slender cypress trees rising above the flat roofs, white buildings shining among the olive trees and terraces falling away into a wall of heat.

§ 2

The white houses of Bethlehem clustered on the hill like a group of startled nuns. They stood on the edge of the road and gazed down into a pit of heat. Where the striped terraces end and the bare rock begins, the last olive trees seemed to be struggling desperately to run back up the stony terraces away from the heat and the sterility of the rock. The white houses watched them with open mouths that were doors, and startled eyes that were windows. And the hot sunlight beat down from the blue sky.

Above the flat, white roofs rose the bell towers of convents and orphanages and monasteries. There was always a bell ringing in the heat. If it was not the bell of the Salesian Fathers, it might be the bell of the Sisters of St.

Vincent de Paul. At the bottom of the road that leads up to this white hill town was a notice board which absurdly pins this region to reality: "Bethlehem Municipal Boundary," it says. "Drive slowly."

As I walked up the hill into Bethlehem, wishing only to be left alone, I was pursued by eager young Arabs in European clothes. They tugged at my sleeve and tried to sell me post cards and books and to lead me into souvenir shops. These little shops sell pious objects carved in mother-of-pearl, in olive wood and in a black stone that comes from the Dead Sea. If these fail to attract the visitor, the pests try to sell him the wedding dress of a Bethlehem woman. When I asked one what he thought I should do with such an embarrassing possession, he smiled winningly and thrust the garments toward me:

"You have no wife?" he said. "Ah, young ladies much like! Very pretty . . . Look, sir . . ."

I tore myself away from these irritating touts and plunged into the dark little lanes of Bethlehem where shops and workshops line part of the main street. They are merely arches open to the road, which is so narrow that the cobbler can sit at his last and chat to his friend, the grocer, on the opposite side of the street.

The people of Bethlehem, who dress like Arabs, are nearly all Christians, and it is believed that they are the descendants of the Crusaders. The married women wear a curious and attractive headdress which certainly reminds one of the Crusades because it is a variation of the tall, foolscap headdress which became fashionable in the early Middle Ages—the cone with a pendant veil which is worn

· 77

by most princesses in fairy tales. When I saw a group of these
women framed by a dark archway, each of them wearing this
headdress, I could easily have imagined myself back in the
times of Richard of the Lion heart.

§ 3

I came to a small gate in a huge stone wall. It was so small
that a boy of twelve would have had to bend down to pass
through it. On the other side was the Church of the Nativity which was built ages ago over the cave and the manger
in which it is believed Jesus was born. This absurd door
is the only entrance to the church. All the others were
blocked up centuries ago to prevent the Moslems from riding into the church on horseback and slaying the Christians.

As I stepped through this door I saw a church that posi-
tively exuded age. Columns of some dull red marble upheld the roof. I was in the church that Constantine built as
a sign that he had become a Christian. I looked around in
amazement, knowing that this building has been standing
for at least one thousand, four hundred years. It was built
above a cave that was believed to be the birthplace of Jesus,
two centuries before Rome became a Christian state.

A service was in progress. At first I thought the choir
was filled with nuns, but they were ordinary Bethlehem
women wearing their tall veiled headdresses.

When the service ended, I walked up the church aisle to
see the Grotto of the Nativity, which is underneath the
high altar. You go down to it by a flight of steps in the
choir. On the way down I had to press myself against

the dark little staircase as two Greek monks, black of eye
and beard, came up swinging a censer of incense.

Fifty-three silver lamps hardly lightened the gloom of the
underground cavern. It was a small cave about fourteen
yards long and only four yards wide. Its walls were covered
with tapestry that reeked of stale incense. When I drew
this tapestry aside to see what was behind it I exposed the
rough smoke-blackened walls of a cave. Gold, silver and
tinsel ornaments gleamed in the pale glow of the fifty-three
lamps.

I thought I was alone until someone moved in the darkness, and I saw a policeman who was on duty to prevent
disputes between the Greek and the Armenian priests. Like
the Church of the Holy Sepulcher, this church at Bethlehem suffers from divided ownership. It is in the hands of
the Latins or Roman Catholics, the Greeks and the Armenians. So careful are these three churches of their rights that
even the sweeping of the dust is sometimes a dangerous
task. There is a column in the church in which there are
three nails. Upon one the Latins may hang a picture, upon
the second the Greeks may do so but the third nail is neutral and no one may hang anything on it! In the floor there
is a star and around it an inscription which reads: "Here
Jesus Christ was born of the Virgin Mary." The removal
of this star a hundred years ago led to a quarrel between
France and Russia which blazed into the Crimean War.

As I stood in the dark pungent cavern I forgot all the
clever and learned things written about the Nativity by pro-
fessors, and I seemed to hear voices singing under a frosty
sky:

· 79

O come, all ye faithful,
Joyful and triumphant,
O come ye, O come ye, to Bethlehem.

How different is that dark little cave under a church from the manger and the stable of one's imagination! As a child I thought of it as a thatched barn with wooden troughs of oats and hay, and a great pile of fodder upon which the Wise Men knelt to adore "the new-born Child." Down the long avenues of memory I seemed to hear the waits singing in the white hush of Christmas night:

While shepherds watched their flocks by night,
All seated on the ground,
The Angel of the Lord came down,
And glory shone around.

There was a rhythmic chinking sound on the stairs. A Greek priest, his black beard curled like that of an Assyrian king, came slowly into the cavern swinging a censer. The incense rolled out in clouds and hung about in the candle flames. He censed the altar and the star. Then, in the most matter-of-fact way, he genuflected and went up into the light of the church.

The cave was suddenly full of little children, silently standing two by two on the stairs. They came forward, knelt down and quickly kissed the stone near the star. Their little faces were very grave in the candlelight. Some of them closed their eyes tightly and whispered a prayer

No sooner had the last of them gone, than I heard the chink-chink of the censer; and into the gloom of the Grotto

80 .

of the Nativity came again a Greek priest like an Assyrian king.

§ 4

There are a number of old houses in Bethlehem built above caves in the limestone rock. These caves are exactly the same as the sacred grotto under the high altar of the Church of the Nativity, and they are probably as ancient. No one who has seen these houses can doubt that Jesus was born in one of them, and not in the stable of European tradition.

I suppose the idea that Christ was born in a stable was suggested by St. Luke's use of the word "manger." To the western mind this word presupposes a stable or a barn, or some outbuilding separate from the house and used as a shelter for animals. But there is nothing in *St. Luke* to justify this.

These primitive houses in Bethlehem gave me an entirely new idea of the scene of the Nativity. They are one-room houses built over caves. Whether these caves are natural or artificial I do not know: they are level with the road, but the room above them is reached by a flight of stone steps, perhaps fifteen or twenty. The caves are used to this day as stables for the animals, which enter from the road level. The family occupies the upper chamber, separated only by the thickness of the rock floor from the cave in which the animals sleep.

It is interesting to remember that the earliest tradition in the Church was that Jesus was born not in a stable or an inn, but in a cave. Justin Martyr, who was born about 100 A.D., repeats a tradition current in his time that, as Joseph had no place in which to lodge in Bethlehem, he discovered a cave near by. But even before Justin's time it seems that the cave below the Church of the Nativity was venerated as the scene of Christ's birth. It is not unreasonable to assume that the caverns below this church were once above ground and formed the bottom stories, or basements, of inhabited houses.

One of the modern cave houses which I visited might have remained unchanged since the time of Christ. The man was attending to the animals, two donkeys and a foal, which were tied up to the rock in the cave. In the room above the woman was sifting some small grain, like millet, through a sieve. From time to time she talked to her husband as he busied himself in the room beneath.

The living room was, like most rooms in the East, bare of furniture. In a corner of it were the matting beds rolled up and tucked away out of sight.

While I was examining the cave houses my American friend, who had taken me through Hezekiah's Tunnel, found me—for we had arranged to meet at Bethlehem—and together we explored the alleyways and the courtyards. We were looking at a Roman mill in a dark stone crypt when a girl came out on a flight of stairs to one side of the courtyard and began talking to us. My friend suddenly turned into an Arab and began pinching the air with his fingers, putting his head on one side and making graceful gestures with his hands.

The girl laughed and he laughed.

"What are you talking about?" I asked.

"I am asking her to let us enter the house," he said. "She has gone to ask her father."

She came out again and leaned over the balcony. She was the loveliest girl I had seen in Palestine. I think she was about eighteen. I was delighted to see that women do still exist in Palestine who justify the rhapsodies of Solomon.

"She says," explained my friend, "that we must wait until the cobbler has gone, because he is a great gossip and it would be all over Bethlehem in five minutes that strange men were received in the house. But we are invited to enter."

So we poked about the yard, pretending to be interested in the old stones, until we saw the cobbler come down the steps holding a pair of old shoes. Then we went up the stairs and entered the house.

There was an outer room, or hall, with a room on each side of it. They were bare of furniture. The family was poor and humble. They worked in the fields. The father was a gray-bearded old Arab in a brown *galabieh,* and the mother was resting on a mat covered with a blanket.

The girl brought in an elder sister and a beautiful little child with yellow hair. We all sat on the floor and my friend chattered away in Arabic as if he had known these people for years. The place rocked with laughter.

"I am," he said, "going to show you what the Bethlehem women wear under their veils. I am asking the elder girl, who is a widow, to put on her wedding dress."

By what process of bare-faced flattery, or by what charm of manner, he was able to do this, I cannot say. But the surprising fact is that the girl, blushing charmingly, disappeared to put on her bridal garments.

"How on earth can you come into a strange house and order people about like this?" I asked.

"Oh," he said, "the Arabs are extraordinarily nice people and so easy to handle if you know how to tackle them."

The younger sister, who, I thought, would make a perfect model for Ruth, entertained us with a bright flow of talk until her sister arrived in her heavily embroidered wedding garments, with her *znekb,* or chain, and the high Bethlehem headdress with its flowing white veil. She readily removed the veil and showed me that the little tower from which it hangs is a small red fez held upright on the head by two cords which tie beneath the chin. All around this little fez are sewn row upon row of coins. The *znekb* hangs from the headdress and contains ten coins with a central pendant.

"Those coins represent a bride's dowry," explained my friend, "and it is possible that they illustrate our Lord's parable of the Lost Coin. You remember how it goes: 'What woman having ten pieces of silver, if she lose one piece, doth not light a candle, and sweep the house, and seek diligently until she find it?' And so on. Now, why should she be so anxious to find one piece out of ten?"

"I have always considered it a tribute to the carefulness of women."

"So have most people. But there is more to it than that. In Jewish times ten drachmas, or ten pieces of silver, were sewn on the headdress of the married woman, and to lose one of them was a terrible reflection on her carefulness and, possibly, on her wifely respect for her husband. It may also have flung her into the superstitious fear into which the loss of a wedding ring will fling a modern wife. That was why the woman in the parable took a lamp and swept the house with such anxiety. . . ."

The family was too poor to offer the usual coffee, but

they made up for it by the charm of their manners and their air of fine breeding. The old man talked to us of the approaching harvest and the poverty of the times. His wife, tired out after a day in the barley fields, talked to us from her bed on the floor.

"I can point out the explanation of another parable to you," said my friend. "You see the matting bed. When an Arab family is young, father, mother, and all the children unroll a large mat and retire to sleep on it, lying together in a row. You remember the Parable of the Stranger. Jesus drew a picture of a man who is aroused, after he has retired to rest, by a friend who asks for three loaves. The man replies that he cannot oblige the stranger for 'the door is now shut and my children are with me in bed; I cannot rise and give thee.' You can see that, like the *fellah* in Palestine to-day, the man in the parable could not get up, once he had gone to bed, without disturbing the entire family."

We said our good-bys and descended the steps. The two girls hung over the balcony, the young one like Ruth and the other in her crusading veil; and their laughter followed us into the little narrow street where the donkeys passed with their loads.

§ 5

I hired a car in Jerusalem and set off one morning to see something more of the Holy Land. I wanted to see Beersheba in the south and then to make my way north to Nazareth and the Sea of Galilee.

I found that the road to Beersheba soon took me into the desert. There were low ridges of hills and cone-shaped "tels" under which lie buried the towns that knew Abraham. Who knows what still lies buried under this desert sand and what wonderful discoveries remain to be made? What could be more exciting, I asked myself, than the life of an archaeologist as he digs down into the bones of dead cities and brings up objects which have not seen the light of the sun for thousands of years?

As my car reeled over a rough track made for camels, boys in sheepskin coats chased goats across the barren land and flocks of sheep wheeled away from the noise of the engine and the dust.

Here and there the desolation was broken by the black goat-hair tents of the Bedouin, a few tethered horses, a few she-camels and their long-legged infants, and perhaps a flock of sheep nosing the burning earth for stray grass.

It is the wild tribal country, with its precious wells, its flocks, its herds and its family feuds, that we know so well from the pages of *Genesis*. It is extraordinary to discover a tract of the earth that has not changed in any essential way since the days of Abraham.

Sheiks like Abraham, with wives like Sarah and sons like Isaac, are still moving from well to well across this hot, parched land. Sons like Esau are jealous of brothers like Jacob, and sometimes even carry into effect the threat in *Genesis:* "Some day I will slay my brother Jacob."

And the road leads on over the wilderness to the little oasis of Beersheba.

There is nothing at Beersheba but a few scattered trees, a mosque, some small shacks, the wells that Abraham knew, a Government house, and a memory of the first World War in a cemetery of British dead: and, in a parched little group of trees, a bust of the British general, Lord Allenby.

The Bedouin who drift into Beersheba to seek tribal justice, or to buy things on credit until the barley harvest is over, admire Lord Allenby, as they admire all warriors; but they hate the bust.

"There has been no good luck," they say, "since the graven image came to Bir es Seba . . ."

For the Allah of the desert Bedouin is in many ways very like the Jehovah of the Old Testament, and the sheik believes firmly and literally in "Thou shalt not make unto thee any graven image, or any likeness of any thing that is in heaven above, or that is in the earth beneath, or that is in the water under the earth."

So if the barley fields are burned up and the rains fail, if the lambs die, if disease smites the goats or the camels, and if death visits the goat-hair tents, the Bedouin always blame the bust of Lord Allenby!

I went to the courthouse with an introduction to the magistrate, who was a magnificent Arab sheik in a flowing robe with a scimitar hanging from his waist. He asked me to sit beside him on the bench while he presided over the weekly court.

We entered an upper room in which about forty Bedouin were talking together. They sat in five main groups at tables. The hot light of the desert was excluded by green wooden blinds. There was a magistrates' bench at one end of the room, and to this the magistrate led me. We took our seats together and surveyed the extraordinary scene.

The group on the floor below us represented a fraction of the week's litigation. Outside in anterooms, all the way down the stairs, in the basement, on the porch outside, and squatting picturesquely near their tethered camels and horses, were the waiting defendants and plaintiffs: for there is nothing the Bedouin loves more than a lawsuit. Law with him is not so much a matter of justice as revenge.

Every week, out of an apparently empty desert, rides this same savage-looking horde of litigants. They come in the best of friends, fight each other with words and impute the most disgraceful motives to each other, but, once the case is settled, go off together in perfect amity.

The law administered in this court is older than many of the books of the Old Testament: it is the old tribal law that was observed in the desert centuries before the children of Israel fled from Egypt.

There were fifteen judges. They were all sheiks of the various local tribes, and were chiefly old men who wore huge, old-fashioned ivory-handled scimitars as a badge of office. Three sheiks judged each case. Five cases usually are argued at once around the little tables in the courthouse, and it is generally possible to polish off about eighty in one day. Now and then, however, they strike a difficult one that, with adjournments, lasts for years.

The fundamental difference between desert law and the law as we know it is that the tribe, and not the individual offender, is held responsible for a crime. And the reason for this is fairly obvious. In the desert of Sinai the criminal can nearly always escape. If you had to punish the individual, you would have to mobilize an army and comb the desert for years in order to put him in the dock! Therefore a criminal brings trouble—for crime is not a disgrace among the Bedouin—first to his tribe and, secondly, to his family.

The commonest offenses are raids on animals, blood feuds or murder, breaches of desert etiquette and disputes about

88 .

A modern Good Samaritan, an Arab, wearing a Western coat and carrying an injured sheep.

A Samarian Madonna today.

land, money and so forth. Women rarely enter the desert courts and crimes against them are practically nonexistent.

The disputes that were being argued below us were varied. One man was suing a friend for having borrowed—not stolen—a sheep. It is the recognized law of the desert that, if a stranger appears at your tent door and your sheep are grazing far away, you are entitled, in order to fulfill the ancient laws of hospitality, to borrow a neighbor's sheep and to slay it in honor of your guest.

Now, a guest is allowed to stay for three days with the Bedouin without question. During that time his life is sacred, and the man whose sheep has been borrowed must not ask for a sheep to replace it. But instantly the guest departs, the man who has borrowed the sheep must, according to desert etiquette, present himself at his friend's tent and say:

"Here is a sheep which I return to you in place of the sheep I took."

If not, he is allowed fourteen days to replace the sheep. Should he fail to do so, he may be obliged to return four sheep.

Another case was one of etiquette. A man had entered another man's tent without permission and gazed upon his neighbor's wife. This was regarded as a serious offence, and everyone was very excited about it. Even the judges seemed angry.

A third case had something to do with a blood feud. These blood feuds exist throughout the desert and nearly every family has one in running order or in temporary suspension. If blood feuds get out of hand they spread like an epidemic of influenza and end in whole tribes having a pitched fight and driving off each other's camels.

Suddenly the arguments around the little tables were interrupted by a violent old Bedouin with a lean face and scanty beard, who rose up and shrieked in fury at the judges. The magistrate hit the bench with a mallet, but the old man rushed forward foaming at the mouth with rage.

It appeared that this old man charged a young Bedouin of the same tribe with the theft of $1,200, which the old man said had been kept in a pot. The defense was that the old man had never had $12 let alone $1,200. Whereupon the old fellow started to scream with rage.

"He is demanding the trial by fire," explained the magistrate. "I do not think we shall allow it in this case."

"You don't mean to say that you permit trial by fire?"

"It is the most respected verdict of all. The whole desert respects the trial by fire," he replied. "The men who administer it are known as *Mobishaa,* and the ordeal itself as *Bishaa.* There are only two such men in all Arabia, one in Sinai and one in the Hedjaz. We employ the man from Sinai.

"The method is this. The *Mobishaa* first asks for a confession. If this is not made, he takes fire and heats an iron in it until it is white hot and covered with white sparks. He then collects his fee! This is $30. Defendant and plaintiff each give him $15, and at the end of the ordeal he returns half the fee to the innocent party.

"The accused steps forward, is given water to wash out his mouth, and is then asked to lick the red-hot iron three times. At the end of this ordeal the *Mobishaa* examines his tongue and gives judgment. It is an extraordinary thing—

and you will think I am romancing—but I have seen men pass unscathed through the ordeal."

"But that can have nothing to do with their guilt or innocence!"

"On the contrary, I believe it has. The guilty man is so terrified that his mouth goes dry and he gets terribly burned. But the innocent man's saliva continues to flow and he does not show anything on his tongue after the ordeal but a redness. Anyhow, the *Mobishaa's* verdict is never questioned. It is the verdict of Allah. . . ."

We went outside and sat in the shade. Two or three of the leading sheiks came around and stood in a dignified, statuesque manner, their hands on the hilts of their swords. Father Abraham, who dug the wells of Beersheba a few yards from where we were sitting, was, I felt, a man just like these tribal chiefs, with the same shrewd but uncomplicated eyes, the same ideas of life and the conduct of life.

§ 6

I motored across the desert and spent the night in camp with a famous archaeologist. I was given a hut to sleep in and warned to keep my shoes and socks off the floor because of the scorpions. We sat on empty biscuit tins and ate a dinner of canned tongue and then by the light of the moon I was shown the ruins of three palaces built one on top of the other.

The first had been built in 3100 B.C., the second in 2500 B.C. and the third, in whose foundations a horse had been sacrificed and buried, in 2200 B.C. There were perfectly

· 91

preserved mud doorways through which Abraham might have walked.

In the morning I was on my way to Ascalon. The road ran for fourteen or fifteen miles through flat, green country. I met the usual strings of camels roped together, slouching along on the edge of the road, and the usual overburdened donkeys. Near El Mejdel I came to a perfect paradise of cultivation and saw, with more attention than one usually gives to such a sight, fields of onions.

Onions have been grown around Ascalon for thousands of years. The Romans liked them and called them *Ascalonium,* from which we get the word *echalote* or, in English, shallot. I had no idea that this historic bulb was still grown there.

When I left the main road and made for the coast, I encountered hundreds of Arabs in brilliant holiday clothes. Every road was thick with them, and they were all making for the seacoast.

There were families mounted on camels and donkeys, the women wearing brilliant blues and reds. I had never before seen so many beautiful girls in Palestine, marred only by the unfortunate fact that they were nearly all cross-eyed. Reaching a slight hill that commands the plain, I saw that for miles around the population, literally in thousands, was making for the seashore at Ascalon. It is an unusual sight to see women and children riding on camels in Palestine, because these animals are always reserved for hard work. But there were thousands of camels, each one with its cargo of little brown children. It was a delightful sight, for the *fellahin* on their frequent feast days let themselves go, put on their gayest clothes, and dance and sing and behave as if they had not one care in the world. Only the camels preserved their impassive superciliousness. Most of them had been shaved and oiled and smeared with mud. This barbering of camels takes place before the great heat sets in.

My first thought that some village feast day was being celebrated was soon banished when I drew nearer to Ascalon. The population of an entire district was streaming down the narrow roads to the sand dunes.

"It is the feast of Nebi Ayub," I learned, after asking perhaps thirty Arabs who could not understand a word of English.

Ayub, I was told, was an ancient prophet who had cured himself of boils by bathing in the sea and, therefore, once a year on his feast day everybody goes to the water. It occurred to me that this Ayub was none other than Job.

The city that was once Ascalon is lost under the sand dunes. The Mediterranean waves break in white foam on miles of magnificent hard sand. Here and there, sticking out of the dunes, are massive old walls of black stone and the ground everywhere is thick with Roman pottery and bits of broken green glass. Among the dunes, near a water wheel turned by a camel who plods around and around in an endless circle, are broken statues that were dug up from the Ascalon that Herod built. What treasures still lie under these gold sand mountains one can only imagine.

I took a narrow path over the dunes and came out on the seashore. One of the most astonishing sights I have ever seen was spread out for miles on the edge of the Mediterranean.

· 93

Hundreds of camels were being given their annual bath. On the sand dunes at the back sat the crowds of women and children who had trekked down from every village in the district: the men and the boys were engaged in the serious process of washing the camels. There was not, of course, one bathing costume among the camel washers, and they looked magnificent as their wet brown bodies caught the sun.

Groups of five or six pulled, prodded and pushed their camels into the breaking waves. Some camels resisted. Some started to kick. Some even broke loose and stampeded back to the women, pursued by wild and angry boys.

On the other hand many of the animals, once they had been persuaded to sit down in the sea, appeared to enjoy themselves. They refused to move! It was as difficult to get them out as it had been to get them in. They sat on the very edge of the sea, with their absurd supercilious heads lifted high above the advancing waves.

As soon as the beasts were settled in the water, naked men rushed at them with knives, with which they scraped off the caked mud. It was a delightful sight, because the camel, like the donkey, does not receive much attention in this life.

I learned afterward that the feast of Nebi Ayub is the only occasion on which the Arab indulges in mixed bathing. In the evening, I was told, thousands of men and women would enter the sea. The women would form little groups apart and run unclothed into the sea. The men would dash in at other parts of the shore.

The Feast of Nebi Ayub seems to be a ceremonial cleansing whose origin is lost in the very mists of time.

94 ·

§ 7

I traveled over a fertile plain dotted with Arab villages hedged about with cactus. The people, so it seemed to me, might have walked out in a body from the pages of the Old Testament. One of the most interesting things about Palestine is that in some districts, notably that south of a line drawn from Jerusalem to Jaffa, the *fellahin* are the descendants of the Canaanites. In feature and habit they bear the signs of their ancient origin. Conquerors have thundered over the land without dislodging them.

I stopped to watch a gardener at work. His land was watered by a series of little channels cut in the soil and dammed by a stopping of earth at various points. Whenever he wanted to irrigate a new portion of garden, he simply lifted his bare foot and kicked away the earth at some point so that the water rushed forward into new places. In this act I recognized the description in *Deuteronomy* of Egypt as a land "where thou sowedst thy seed, and *wateredst it with thy foot,* as a garden of herbs."

Every little hill carried on its crest a village whose name is known to millions of people, the little villages of the Old Testament. They looked like rows of mud boxes ranged in lines around a hilltop. Girls with water pots on their shoulders walked through fields of growing barley, and beside the road stood little boys like young David, fitting smooth pebbles into the bags of their slings. I have never until now felt sorry for Goliath! But, with all his size and strength, he must have had about as much chance against David and his sling as a man with a spear would have against a modern gunman. The sling, when wielded by a practiced hand can be a deadly weapon.

One has to visit Palestine to understand how accurate is the Bible. It has become the fashion to say that the Old Testament is a collection of Jewish fables, and I am sure some young people today imagine that men like Saul and David never existed. Not only did they exist, but today there are men whose lives and outlook are exactly the same. You meet them on every road. The Bible is the most accurate of all guides to the life of modern Palestine. Let me give an instance.

I stopped at a humble little village. I do not know the name of it. In a clearing several women sat beside a black pot beneath which blazed the thorn bushes that grow all over Palestine. As the thorns burned they made a crackling, splitting sound, and I realized the descriptive power of that famous line in *Ecclesiastes:* "As the crackling of thorns under a pot, so is the laughter of the fool."

In the fields around this village men were unconsciously illustrating the Bible. One man was guiding a plow drawn by an ox and a camel. This is unfair on the smaller animal. The wooden yoke sinks from the high camel to the low ox so that he bears more than his share of the weight, and this clumsy arrangement chafes the necks of both animals.

Is not this exactly what St. Paul meant in his Second Epistle to the Corinthians: "Be ye not unequally yoked together with unbelievers: for what fellowship hath righteousness with unrighteousness, and what communion hath light with darkness?"

A little farther on was another plowman. He drove a restless, difficult ox. The beast was not broken in to the

96 .

The city of Tiberias as it appears today, with the Sea of Galilee in the background.

Ruins of the Synagogue in Capernaum.   All that remains of Herod's Judgment Hall in Sebaste.

plow. He lowered his head and tried to back. The plow-man carried in his hand a pointed stick used for scraping the earth from the plowshare. Whenever the ox grew diffi-cult he prodded him with the spike, and I knew that I was seeing something that Jesus had seen and noticed as He walked the roads of Palestine.

"Saul, Saul," cried Jesus, "why persecutest thou me? It is hard for thee to kick against the pricks."

But the most interesting, and the most Biblical sight on the roads of Palestine is the shepherd. You see him every-where. He comes along at the head of his flock, generally carrying over his shoulders a lamb or an injured sheep.

He is a man burned almost black by exposure to the sun. He wears the flowing Bedouin head veil, the *keffiyeh*, bound with two black twisted cords known as the *agaal*. Be-neath his robes he often wears a sheepskin coat with the fleece turned next to the body. He is one of the many char-acters who walk the roads of Palestine exactly as they must have done in the time of Jesus.

A most remarkable thing is the sympathy that exists be-tween him and his flock. He never drives them as our own shepherds drive their sheep. He always walks at their head, leading them along the roads and over the hills to new pas-ture: and, as he goes, he sometimes talks to them in a loud singsong voice, using a weird language unlike anything I have ever heard in my life. The first time I heard this sheep and goat language I was on the hills at the back of Jericho. A goatherd had descended into a valley and was mounting the slope of an opposite hill when, turning around, he saw his goats had remained behind to devour a rich patch of scrub. Lifting his voice, he spoke to the goats in a language

· 97

that Pan must have spoken on the mountains of Greece. It was uncanny because there was nothing human about it. The words were animal sounds arranged in a kind of order. No sooner had he spoken than an answering bleat shivered over the herd, and one or two of the animals turned their heads in his direction. But they did not obey him. The goatherd then called out one word and gave a laughing kind of whinny. Immediately a goat with a bell around his neck stopped eating and, leaving the herd, trotted down the hill, across the valley and up the opposite slopes. The man, accompanied by this animal, walked on and disappeared around a ledge of rock. Very soon a panic spread among the herd. They forgot to eat. They looked up for the shepherd. He was not to be seen. They became conscious that the leader with the bell at his neck was no longer with them. From the distance came the strange laughing call of the shepherd, and at the sound of it the entire herd stampeded into the hollow and leaped up the hill after him.

I would like to know what an English sheep dog would make of the Palestine sheep, because our principle of droving is something that neither Arab shepherds nor their sheep dogs understand. It is all done by word of mouth, and the sheep follow their shepherds like dogs. The Arab sheep dog is used therefore not to drive sheep but to protect them against thieves and wild animals.

Early one morning I saw an extraordinary sight. Two shepherds had evidently spent the night with their flocks in a cave. The sheep were all mixed together and the time had come for the shepherds to go in different directions. One of the shepherds stood some distance from the sheep and began to call. First one, then another, then four or five animals ran toward him; and so on until he had counted his whole flock.

More interesting than the sight of this was the knowledge that Jesus must have seen exactly the same sight and described it in His own words:

"He calleth his own sheep by name, and leadeth them out. And when he putteth forth his own sheep, he goeth before them, and the sheep follow him: for they know his voice. And a stranger they will not follow, but will flee from him: for they know not the voice of strangers. This parable spake Jesus unto them. . . . I am the good shepherd, and know my sheep and am known of mine."

It is with a feeling of delight that one realizes how many things in the Gospels which one has regarded as figures of speech are literal descriptions of the things that were happening around Jesus and His disciples as they walked the roads of Palestine. The ordinary sights are so frequently mentioned by Jesus that I believe many of His sayings and parables were suggested by the things that were happening around Him as He was speaking. Whenever I read the Gospels now, I always imagine Him pointing out something, as He undoubtedly pointed to a field of flowers when He said, "Consider the lilies of the field," and as He may have pointed to a shepherd calling his sheep together before He expounded the parable I have just quoted from St. John.

One reason why the sheep and the shepherd are on such familiar terms in the Holy Land is that sheep are kept

· 99

chiefly for wool and milk, and therefore live longer and exist together as a flock for a considerable time. Also the Shepherd spends his life with them. He is with them from their birth onward, day and night, for even when they are driven into a cave or a sheepfold for the night, he never leaves them.

In the time of Jesus sheep must have been even more numerous than they are today. The Temple sacrifices demanded an incredible number of them. When Solomon dedicated the Temple he sacrificed a hundred and twenty thousand sheep. Enormous droves, destined to be offered on the altar, were always moving along the roads of ancient Palestine. The shepherds at Bethlehem during the birth of Christ were, no doubt, men keeping guard over a sacrificial flock from the well-known Migdal Eder, the "watch tower of the flock."

The species has not varied since the time of Moses. It is a peculiar type of sheep and I have never seen any other like it. Its distinctive feature is a broad, fat tail, or, more correctly, rump. This grows to such an enormous size that, I am told, it has often to be tied up along the sheep's back. I think Herodotus was the first writer to mention that sometimes the shepherds make little wheeled carts to carry these tails! I have never seen one and neither have residents in Palestine whom I have questioned.

The weight of these fat tails is, I believe, extraordinary. I have read that some of them weigh twenty pounds and that a sheep weighing sixty pounds has been known to possess a tail weighing twenty. The fat is something between butter and lard, and the Bedouin regard it as a great delicacy. In this, as in their other habits, they faithfully reproduce the life of the Old Testament. The fat tail was included in the "rump" that is mentioned in the Old Testament. In *Exodus* it is laid down that "Thou shalt take of the ram the fat and the rump," and in *Leviticus* it is ordered that the officiating priest must take off "the whole rump . . . hard by the backbone." It was Jehovah's special delicacy.

There are two interesting references to sheep—or rather rams and lambs—in the Psalms:

"The mountains skipped like rams, and the little hills like lambs."

"The voice of the Lord breaketh the cedars: yea, the Lord breaketh the cedars of Lebanon.

"He maketh them also to skip like a calf; Lebanon and Sirion like a young unicorn."

I suppose nobody would take these references literally and imagine that these animals actually skipped, or that, if so, the skipping was anything more than the high spirits which are sometimes associated with lambs in springtime, but rarely with the rams. But did the Israelites, I wonder, teach their flocks to skip and dance? If so, a new significance is given to the above verses. I ask this because I have come across a strange account of dancing sheep in an account written in 1745 by a missionary in Palestine named Stephen Schultz.

He describes how he was entertained in a Bedouin camp on the Plain of Esdraelon and how the women set up a chorus of praise in his honor as, in fact, they do to this day when a guest arrives. Meanwhile, in compliment to the guests, the flocks were paraded under their several shepherds.

"Besides this shouting for joy in the women's tent," wrote Schultz, "the sheep are led through the men's tent. It was done in the following manner: the shepherd went on in front and had a shepherd's pipe or flute, upon which he played, and the sheep followed him. As the shepherd modulated the tone when piping, by raising, lowering or letting it run fast or slowly, the sheep made the same movements, and as accurately as a French dancer would do whilst following a minuet.

When one shepherd had passed in such a manner with his sheep, another followed with his flock; and so one after the other, during which progress the skipping of the lambs and he-goats drew special attention. Not all the shepherds had flutes, but some of them had other musical instruments.

"The dance of the sheep, he-goats and lambs being ended, the camels came. They, however, had not to dance through the hut, but round it. While this skipping of the animals was going on, the tongue-rattling of the women was often heard."

Has this extraordinary custom died out completely or does it still linger, as so many Old Testament customs do, among the Bedouin in the remote desert? No one who has seen the authority exercised by the Arab shepherd over his flocks, or the obedience of the sheep to their shepherd, can doubt that this pretty trick could be possible.

No animal mentioned in the Bible can compare in symbolical interest with the sheep. I believe it is mentioned over five hundred times. And you cannot go very far along the roads in Palestine without encountering the figure who, staff in hand, symbolizes the love and compassion of Jesus Christ.

CHAPTER FOUR

I stay awhile at Nazareth and watch the village carpenter at work. I go on into Galilee where I stay at Tiberias. I meet the fishermen of Galilee and go fishing with them on the lake.

§ 1

Some instinct warned me to stop on the hill that runs up into Nazareth. I looked back to the south over a sweep of country that recalls much of the sorrows and triumphs of a nation.

I saw the great Plain of Esdraelon stretching like a smooth, green sea to the distant hills of Samaria. The shadows of the clouds moved over it as if the ghosts of old armies were crossing the haunted plain. There are over twenty battlefields down there. The level arena has known the thunder of chariots from Egypt, Assyria and Babylon. Somewhere on the plain, Barak smote the Canaanites. From its green levels Gideon drove the Midianites toward the Jordan. On the hills at the back Saul went by night to consult the Witch of Endor, and by day saw his armies scattered and his sons slain. It was down there, too, that the dead body of Josiah was hurried from the triumphant Egyptians and borne in sorrow to Jerusalem.

The brown hills to the south, the hills of Samaria, had known the denunciatory figure of Elijah. They had heard his burning words and seen the prophetic fire in his eyes. On the skyline was the hill that held Naboth's Vineyard and

the hill on which Jezebel met death. To the right the long
calm ridge of Carmel cut the sky, and I looked at it remem-
bering the priests of Baal and the fire that Elijah drew down
from heaven to confound them.

When I had looked my fill at this tremendous map of
Old Testament history, I went on through Nazareth; and
the road ran upward to the top of another hill. There I
stopped; for down below me to the northward lay a new
world—Galilee.

I do not know the name of this hill, but I shall always
think of it as the Hill of the Two Testaments. To the south
lies the Old Testament; to the north lie Galilee and the
New. As I looked northward to the new land, the idea came
to me that this hill reproduces in nature the title page
which printers of the Bible place between the books of the
prophets and the life of Christ. And I thought that although Jesus may not have visited all the places which are
now called holy, there can be no doubt that He must have
often stood on this hill as a boy. He must have known all
His nation's ghosts, which crowd up from the south, and He
must have looked with affection toward the calm and lovely
north and the road that runs down over the mountains to
the lake.

One pictures Him in imagination rising from the hill as
the sun drops into the sea and going down through the hush
of the twilight to Nazareth. Night is closing in on the Plain
of Esdraelon and the hills of Samaria are already in shadow.
But the last thing that fades from sight on the plain below
is a white streak. It is the road that goes on through
Samaria and through the wilderness of Judea to end at last
far to the south before the gates of Jerusalem.

§ 2

As the road sweeps across the broad green plain and
climbs into the mountains on which Nazareth is enthroned
the visitor can think of nothing but the boyhood of Jesus.
Every rock and every hill is important, for these things do
not change and He must have known these rocks and these
hills. Looking back, the great plain stretching to the sky
and the outward thrust spur of Carmel to the west are in-
tensely significant.

When the road straightens out at the top of the hill and
runs toward the snow-white houses of Nazareth toward the
thousands of spearlike cypresses, the terraces of fig and olive
trees, the town is exactly as one likes to imagine it. Even
Bethlehem is not more satisfying to the eye. But, even while
a stranger's car approaches, children hold out their hands
greedily from the roadside, and the awful cry *"Baksheesh"*
comes down the wind. On arrival, there is a rush for the
unfortunate victim.

Small waspish children crowd around, shouting *"Baksheesh"* at the tops of their voices, while various unpleasant
persons thrust out post cards, murmuring "Pictures of the
Virgin's Fountain, very cheap": and among those who run
toward the stranger and pull him by the sleeve are old
women with trays of lace, who leave in his hand cards which
read: "Dear friend! Will you kindly give this to shop or to
a person who likes to deal with me in needlework, and
thank you for your favor. Forget me not!"

It may be childish to be furious because one's picture of
Nazareth is spoiled by a horde of noisy people, and because
arrival in one of the few towns on earth which should be

106 .

holy is made horrible by every kind of mean huckster trading on the sacredness of the place, and by touts who offer to take you "to the house where Jesus lived" as touts offer to take you around the sights of Cairo. I don't think so. There are some places in this world which should be grave and quiet and lovely.

One is shown all kinds of holy places in Nazareth, but perhaps the only one that really convinces is the Virgin's Fountain. This is, and ever has been, the only water supply of Nazareth. The stream gushes out of the mountain and runs through a conduit to a public fountain where women fill fuel cans with water all day long. The Greeks have built a church above the source of this spring and, when you go down into the darkness of this sanctuary, you can hear the water bubbling up from the rock. This must be the spring from which the Virgin Mary drew water.

Down in the narrow streets of the town I found a whole street of carpenters busily at work sawing wood, and using planes and chisels. These men, who work in archways open to the street, are mostly Christian Arabs, and a characteristic product of the trade is a wooden cradle on rockers which is common all over Galilee. These cradles are always painted blue, a color which is believed to ward off evil spirits.

As one stands among the wood shavings of these little shops in Nazareth, the old question: "Did Jesus work at the carpenter's bench?" comes to one's mind. St. Mark calls Him "the carpenter," but St. Matthew, "the carpenter's son." An attempt has often been made, by an examination of the similes used by Jesus, to prove that He was a practical carpenter during the years of His life of which we know nothing. But these references are too slender for anyone, except a Biblical critic, to found an opinion.

There are His sayings: "Cleave the wood and there you will find me"; "If they do these things in a green tree, what shall be done in the dry"; and there is the similitude of the mote and the beam. Surely to these we might add the parable of the house built upon sand?

I was interested to discover that the carpenters of modern Nazareth are of two kinds: the modern carpenter, who makes furniture and prepares wood for the builder, and the old-fashioned carpenter.

If Jesus did adopt the trade of Joseph, we must imagine Him working as the old-fashioned carpenters of Nazareth work today. The methods have not changed.

Their clients are the small farmers and the agricultural laborers of the district. They contract to make, and to keep in repair for a year, all the agricultural tools of a village. Payment is made in grain, so much for each yoke of oxen. At the end of the year the village carpenter goes around at threshing time to all his clients and draws his pay in barley, wheat, sesame or olives.

In the old days these carpenters had more work to do. They used to make doors and window frames from the dwarf oaks of Bashan, a wood called by the Arabs, *Siindian*. But this branch of their work has been monopolized by the modern craftsmen, who can do much cheaper carpentry in Austrian pine.

I came to one dark little hovel in which a very old man, squatting on the floor among a pile of aromatic wood chips and shavings, was using a primitive hand drill. Round about him were various yokes and plows and agricultural tools. He was the real old-fashioned carpenter of Palestine, a character who has existed unchanged since the invasion of the Israelites.

While I was exploring the street of the carpenters, I recalled a rather significant remark of Justin Martyr, who wrote that Jesus, "when amongst men, worked as a carpenter, making ploughs and yokes, thus teaching the marks of righteousness and making an active life."

There is an ancient and curious legend to the effect that the Emperor Julian, the apostate who tried to crush Christianity and bring back the pagan gods, once asked a Christian: "What is the Carpenter doing now?" And the Christian answered, "He is making a coffin." The point of the anecdote is that Julian died soon afterward.

There seem, among the early Christians, to have been some men who believed that Jesus practiced the craft, and others who, piously considering that such humble work lowered His dignity, attempted to disguise the fact. But there can be little doubt that Joseph the Carpenter was exactly like the village carpenters in Galilee today, whose skill ministers to a whole village and whose reward comes at harvest time.

§ 3

Galilee is one of the sweetest words I know. Even were it possible to dissociate it from the Ministry of Jesus, it would still be a lovely word whose three syllables suggest the sound of lake water lapping a shore. It is as soft as the word Judea is hard, as gentle as Judea is cruel. It is not necessary to visit the Holy Land to appreciate the rocky harshness of

"Judea" or to hear the water falling from the oars in "Galilee."

The meaning of the word Galilee is "Ring, or Region, of the Gentiles." The Hebrew word *Galîl* means a circlet, or anything that is round. Chanctonbury Ring and the Links of Forth convey the same idea in English. The district was never entirely Jewish, even in the earliest times. Ten cities of Galilee were given by Solomon to Hiram, King of Tyre, as part payment for the building of the Temple, and the invasion of the Gentile population continued in later times. When Jesus went to live beside Galilee, the western shore of the lake was dotted with a ring of towns and fishing villages in which the non-Jewish element was very strong. The pure-blooded Orthodox Jew of Jerusalem looked down with contempt upon the Galilean and made fun of his dialect and of the way he pronounced the gutturals. Those who stood in the court of the High Priest's house after the arrest of Jesus detected that St. Peter was a follower of Christ. "Thou art a Galilean," they said, "for thy speech betrayeth thee." Amusing errors in grammar and absurd mistakes due to mispronunciation were constantly cited by the superior Judeans as proof of the stupid, hillbilly character of the Galileans.

It seems, however, that in freeing itself from the Rabbinic rigidity of Judea, Galilee found room for idealism and an intense nationalism. While the Judean had bound himself up in formalism, the Galilean had become speculative and independent. It was not chance that led Jesus to sow the seeds of His teaching on the receptive shores of Galilee. . . .

Now, when the time came for me to set out for the Sea of Galilee, I found myself almost nervously apprehensive.

Would it be cheapened by competitive piety, as many parts of Palestine have been cheapened? Would there be anything left to remind a man of Christ? I did not know. I was conscious only of the fact that Galilee must be the supreme adventure in any journey to the Holy Land. Above all places on the earth, it is the one most closely associated with Jesus Christ, and whenever the lovely word is spoken it calls up a picture of Him, not yet the Christ of whom St. Paul preached, but the Jesus of our inmost hearts who called little children to His knee and preached the gospel of love and compassion to the humble, the simple and the heavy laden.

§ 4

As I went down into Galilee, I learned something about the Gospels that I could never have known if I had not visited the Holy Land. Nazareth is a frontier post between the north and the south. To go into Galilee is to turn one's back on the arena of the Old Testament, and there is something in the formation of the land that gives a feeling of finality to the act: one cannot possibly go into Galilee without the knowledge that one has definitely said farewell to Judea. It is not until one crosses this Hill of the Two Testaments that one's mind shakes itself free from the powerful hypnotism of Jerusalem.

By going into Galilee Jesus performed a symbolic act. He turned His back on the world of the Old Testament, and from the moment of that turning away the New Testament begins.

Everyone must feel how different are these two worlds. In the New Testament we seem to have emerged from a dark, fierce eastern world into a clear light that is almost European. In fact Rome is already in sight. The center of the Old Testament world is rigid, exclusive Jerusalem; the center of the New Testament world is international Galilee, a country crossed in the time of Christ by the great military roads from the north and by the ancient caravan routes from the east, a country in which a man seen in the distance might be an imperial messenger riding to Caesarea with tidings of the Emperor's death, or a tax-gatherer from the main road to Damascus, or a Greek architect on his way to build a new theater in Jerash in the Decapolis.

The busy international corridor was the place in which Jesus taught. He alone of all the prophets who had come out of Israel deliberately cut Himself off from the theological stronghold of Judea. And the roads He chose to tread were not the roads of the priests and the rabbis but the roads of the world. So in the road that runs over a hill from Nazareth to the Sea of Galilee a man detects the first promise of Christianity.

The road runs down toward a green valley enclosed by gentle hills. Brown hawks hang in the air, watching the earth. Now and then one drops like a stone out of the sky and is up and away again in a flash. Tumbled rocks, in which thorn and cactus grow, line the road and slope down to the valley; and in this green valley is a trickle of water. After the thirsty highlands of Judea, where every drop of rain is saved in cisterns, the sound of running water is luxurious and extravagant. The blue iris that grows in wet places seems almost spendthrift.

To the left is a straggling brown town on a hill with a

crusaders' castle on the top, ruined but still dominant. Half-way down the hill is a pitiful dead village called Raineh, which has never recovered from the earthquake of 1927. Its houses still lie in ruins and its walls have fallen down. If anyone wants to know what a biblical town must have looked like after it had been conquered by warriors like Saul or David, let him go and look at Raineh.

At the foot of the hill is a small impoverished Arab village. Bare hills interspersed with sparse wheat fields surround it; beyond lies a wide green plain which the pilgrims of the Middle Ages believed to be the place where Jesus gathered the ears of wheat on the Sabbath.

The little village is called Kefr Kenna, which scarcely disguises the name of Cana of Galilee, where Jesus turned the water into wine at the marriage feast.

There are two churches in Cana, one a simple Greek church and the other an archaeological Franciscan church. In the first a fat Greek priest shows you two stone urns which he tells you are the very water jars of the miracle. One of them, I believe, was a baptismal font in an eighteenth-century church and the other, I understand, is no older than the sixteenth century. When you express doubt about these relics, the fat priest shrugs his shoulders. The kindest thing one can think about him is that he probably believes in them himself.

The Franciscan church, on the other hand, is interesting. It is built on the site of an ancient church which was standing in 726 A.D., and I have no doubt that tradition says that it stands on the spot occupied by the house of the wedding feast.

The road bends around past Cana and plunges again

into the hills. Suddenly you see, lying a thousand feet below, a strip of bright blue. It is your first sight of the Sea of Galilee. As you sometimes look upward in a mountain gorge and see a strip of blue sky shining, so in this place you look downward through a gorge to a distant strip of water as blue as any sky. This first sight of the Sea of Galilee is one of the most sacred memories of Palestine.

The road begins to run steadily downhill. The air grows hotter. You are reminded of the heat of the Jordan Valley. You continue to descend into the hot trench and at the end of the road—seven hundred feet below sea level—you come to the palms, the greenness, the blue lake water, and the white roofs of Tiberias.

§ 5

The little hotel in Tiberias stands near the lake. I have discovered that whenever one arrives in a hotel in Palestine it is a good idea to follow the stairs right to the top. There is always a flat roof that gives an excellent general view of whatever town one may happen to be in. I came out on a space as large as a tennis court, so white and dazzling that I could see nothing until I had put on sun glasses. Then I looked down on Tiberias.

I saw hundreds of flat-roofed white houses marching down a gentle hill slope to stand in picturesque confusion on the lake side. Little white domes varied the rectangular uniformity of the white roofs. Here and there a minaret like a Georgian pepper pot stood up higher than domes or roofs. There was one dark, narrow main street from which hundreds of squalid little lanes radiated, and this street was congested with men, women, children, camels and donkeys. The background was a high green mountain with a few houses dotted about its slopes.

In front of me the Sea of Galilee lay ruffled by a slight wind. It was not a uniform color. There were patches of dark and light blue and also touches of pale green. The lake is heart-shaped, with the narrowest part to the south. It is thirteen miles long and at its widest part about seven miles across. Mountains rise all around it. On the western shore they are green mountains; on the eastern shore they are the brown barren precipices of the desert, part of the rocky barrier that rises east of the Jordan and marches south with the river, past the Dead Sea down to the Gulf of Akaba. When I looked to the north I saw the sight that impresses itself upon the mind of all who live in Galilee: I saw a magnificent ridge of mountain covered with snow. It stood up like a screen to the north. The snow never melts in its deepest corries even in the height of summer. It was Mount Hermon, the Mountain of the Transfiguration.

What makes it so impossible to compare the Sea of Galilee with any European lake is the subtropical climate. It is seven hundred feet below sea level and, like its companion lake, the Dead Sea, many miles due south, it belongs to a different latitude from the rest of Palestine. The mountains that rise all around it have their heads in a temperate climate and their feet in a lake around whose shores banana, palm, bamboo and sugarcane thrive. But the water of the Sea of Galilee is fresh, not salt and bitter like that of the Dead Sea.

The second thing that impresses one about the Sea of Galilee is its desolation. It is, with the exception of the white town of Tiberias, a deserted lake. Through field glasses one can see, far off along the western bank toward the north, a dark clump of eucalyptus trees which are supposed to mark the site of Bethsaida, and next to them a small white building and more trees which stand where Capernaum is believed to have stood. You see uneasy mounds of black stones near the shore which are the dead bones of old cities. When you look at the pink and mauve hills opposite, you see that they are wild and desolate, slashed with brown thirsty valleys as with the slashes of knives. Dotted about them here and there are little black squares, sometimes near the shore but more often higher on the hills. They are the goat-hair tents of Bedouin tribes.

But the Sea of Galilee, even in its desolation, breathes an exquisite peace and a beauty that surpass anything in Palestine. The landscape has altered in detail since Jesus made His home in Capernaum, but the broad outline has not changed. The hills are the hills He looked upon, the lights and shadows that turn the Gergesene heights to gold and purple, the little breezes that whip the lake into whiteness, the blue water that fades to a milky green where the Jordan enters at the north; none of these has changed. These are the things that Jesus looked upon and loved when He lived in Galilee.

§ 6

I went into the streets of Tiberias. It is a shabby, squalid little town and crouches like a beggar on the lake side. It is a town of rags and dark eyes and dark cellars, of little jumbled shops and narrow streets. The ruins of a fine crusading wall of black basalt, in whose bastions families live in unspeakable poverty, rise from the water's edge.

The Herodian ruins lie a little way to the south of the modern town. Only a few rubble walls exist to speak of the town that Herod built to minister to his summer palace on the hill. Part of the three-mile wall can still be traced, but stretches of it have fallen into the lake. The hill at the back is pitted and scarred with ruins. High up on its slopes are mounds, shattered pillars and old masonry, which mark the site of the palace of Antipas. From the side of this hill I picked out all kinds of Roman pottery and small fragments of iridescent glass.

One relic of Roman times is still alive. From a hill near the lake gushes a stream of hot mineral water. This spring, which is claimed to give the same water as that of Carlsbad, and was mentioned by Pliny, was known and valued in the earliest times. No doubt Vespasian and Titus bathed in it when they carried the war into Galilee. And it is still healing the woes of humanity. I visited a large bathing house to which patients come from all parts of Syria, Palestine and Trans-Jordan.

§ 7

Rising at the exquisite hour of 4 A.M., when the world is hushed and cool, I went up to the roof of the hotel to watch the sun rise over the Lake of Galilee.

At this time Tiberias is covered with a shroud of silence and grayness. An Arab, who picked himself from the dust where he had spent the night, stole off into the morning stillness like a ghost.

There was one star still burning in the sky. Beyond the

flat roofs of the intervening houses the Sea of Galilee was lying cold and gray like an old mirror, unruffled by any wind of dawn. On the opposite bank the savage Gergesene hills halted at the water's edge like crouching beasts. Behind those hills a faint pink glow filled the sky, growing every second more powerful; it widened and spread, quenching the last star, and giving, even before the sun rose, the thinnest shadows to palm trees and houses.

Men and animals knew that a new day had come. Cocks crowed in a chorus that was echoed from hill to hill. Arabs, their heads still shrouded in their robes, for they sleep fully dressed, led camels and donkeys to water. Sparrows sent up an excited chirping, and swifts filled the air with their bright screaming.

Then suddenly the sun leaped over the hills of Gergesa and—everything was changed! It was warm. The lake was blue. I could see the snow shining on Hermon to the north. The bells of the Greek convent set up a deep ringing. There was a smell of cooking from somewhere. And the muezzin came out on the minaret of the mosque and called the faithful to prayer. So a new day came to Tiberias.

I wandered in the early morning on the hill where the palace of Herod Antipas once shone in a glory of marble and gold. I looked down on the Sea of Galilee, blue under the morning sun. Sometimes I saw a white sail leaning against the wind, moving to the north, where the best fish are caught just where the milky-green Jordan flows into the lake. But more often there are no sails. There is only blue water lying still in the windless heat and a shore curving around to the north, with Magdala, Bethsaida and Caper-

118 .

naum lying in the hollow of the curve. Peace lies like a benediction over the Sea of Galilee: the peace of silence, of solitude, of memory.

§ 8

I went down to the little jetty one morning and arranged to go for a day's fishing on the Sea of Galilee.

The boat was a large, clumsy affair manned by four fishermen who took it in turns to row with oars as thick as cart shafts. There was a sail lying in the bottom of the boat, ready to go up in the unlikely event of a breeze. So we set off in burning sunlight over a still, blue lake.

About sixty men earn their living on the Sea of Galilee by following the trade of St. Peter. They were all Arabs and are mostly Moslems. The fishing nets used on the lake are of three kinds: the hand-net, or *shabakeh;* the draw-net, or *jarf;* and the floating-net, or *m'batten.* The first two are the most popular. The hand-net is used all over the lake, but the draw-net is employed chiefly in the Jordan estuary at the north end.

While two of the fishermen rowed, the other two sat in the boat preparing their nets. These were circular and of very fine mesh, weighed down on the outer edge with dozens of small leaden weights. They are flung by hand and are evidently the same kind as those mentioned in the Gospels. The disciples, when first called by Jesus, were "casting" their nets.

The youngest of the fishermen spoke quite fair English, and from him I learned that fishing on the Lake of Galilee is not a very profitable business.

"We go out all night and catch our fish," he said, "but in the morning we get only a few piasters for them. But the merchant, he get many, many piasters. . . ."

And my mind sped northward, far from the sunny waters of Galilee, to the cold North Sea and to the pilchard fleet of Cornwall, where so often I have heard the same complaint against the middleman; it is the eternal cry of the fisherman.

There was not a breath of wind. The sky was blue. But Abdul, the young fisherman, sniffed the air and, looking to the south, said that a storm was coming. This is, and always has been, one of the peculiarities of the Lake of Galilee. Sudden storms swoop swiftly over this low-lying sheet of water whipping the surface of the lake with fury and covering it with waves that frequently swamp the small row boats. The reason is that winds from the west passing over the highlands come swirling down through a hundred gorges and narrow valleys into the deep pit in which the lake lies. The water is smooth one moment and the next it is a raging sea in which men battle for life. Three men had recently been drowned in such a storm, said Abdul, and their bodies had not yet been recovered.

It is one of these storms that is described so vividly in the Gospels.

"And, behold, there arose a great tempest in the sea, insomuch that the ship was covered with the waves; but He was asleep.

"And His disciples came to Him, and awoke Him, saying, Lord, save us: we perish.

"And He saith unto them, Why are ye fearful, O ye of little faith? Then He arose, and rebuked the winds and the sea; and there was a great calm."

How lovely it was on this hot morning, the shores receding, no sound but the creak of the huge oars, the splash of the water and the little Arab songs that one of the men would sing, softly humming a verse that would lead to a shouted chorus.

We made for the opposite bank, where the hills of Gergesa seemed even more terrible and inhospitable as we drew nearer. They looked as they must have looked in the time of Christ: thirsty, burned-up hills scored with thousands of thin slashes, the marks of dried-up torrents, and invaded by dark gullies in which no man would venture unarmed.

How faithfully the Gospels paint the characteristics of this country. Even today, after a lapse of nearly two thousand years, this country of the Gergesenes is the place in which one would expect to meet a madman.

It was from one of those fearful precipices that the Gadarene swine stampeded into the lake. Has it ever occurred to you to wonder why swine, an unholy beast to the Jew, should have been feeding around the Sea of Galilee? Tucked away in these hills are the ruins of Greek cities which flourished in the time of Jesus, the cities of the Greek-speaking Decapolis. And they had no prejudice against pork.

We jumped ashore and clambered over the hot rocks. There were three or four Bedouin tents pitched near by. The Bedouin were poor, hungry-looking people. The whole tribe turned to look at us, staring with the uncompromising intensity of animals.

A few minutes' walk from the encampment brought us to a wild little valley in which a few strips of barley were growing. Here we saw an old Bedouin crouched on the ground, eating grass.

"He is hungry," commented Abdul, "and has nothing else to eat."

"But the lake is full of fish," I said. "Why doesn't he catch some?"

This seemed to puzzle Abdul. He shrugged his shoulders.

"The Bedouin do not catch fish," he said.

The sight of the man's poverty depressed me so much that I performed the usual act of a sympathetic European and gave him some money. But what use was it to him? In order to buy anything with it he would have to cross the lake to Tiberias, or else walk about thirty miles into the mountains. A more valuable gift to him than any amount of money would have been a sandwich.

Poor Nebuchadnezzar! He looked at the coin in his palm and thanked me; then, with the innate politeness of the desert Arab, he bent down and swiftly plucked some long blades of grass, which he pressed into my hands. It was all he had to offer.

We rowed off again and set our course for the supposed ruins of Capernaum. This town, like all the lake-side villages which were so well known to Jesus, has disappeared from the map. Many archaeologists, however, believe that its site is marked by a mound of ruins lying on the eastern bank of the lake; a fine synagogue was recently discovered here and has been as far as possible rebuilt.

There is a grove of eucalyptus trees through which the synagogue shines like a small Roman temple. Many people believe that this is the ruin of the synagogue in which Jesus preached. Within ten minutes by boat from Capernaum is a little bay which is said to mark the site of Bethsaida, and next to it is a squalid huddle of Arab houses called el Mejdel, the supposed site of Magdala, the town of Mary Magdalene.

We beached the boat in a desolate little bay. One of the fishermen girded his garments to the waist and waded into the lake with his nets draped over his left arm. He stood waiting, as if watching for a movement in the water. Then, with a swift overarm motion, he cast the hand-net. It shot through the air and descended on the water like a ballet dancer's skirt when she sinks to the ground. The dozens of little lead weights carried the bell-shaped net through the water, imprisoning any fish within its area.

But time after time the net came up empty. It was a beautiful sight to see him casting. Each time the neatly folded net belled out in the air and fell so precisely on the water that the small lead weights hit the lake at the same moment, making a thin circular splash.

While he was waiting for another cast, Abdul shouted to him from the bank to fling to the left, which he instantly did. This time he was successful. He waded out and felt around with his feet. Then he drew up the net and we could see fish struggling in it. I was interested in this, because the fishermen were unconsciously repeating one of the most wonderful incidents in the Gospels.

Jesus appeared to seven disciples after the Resurrection. He stood on the shores of the lake at dawn and cried:

"Children, have ye any meat?"

They answered Him, "No."

"Cast the net on the right side of the ship, and ye shall find," He said.

They cast as Jesus had directed and "drew the net to land full of great fishes, an hundred and fifty and three: and for all there were so many, yet was not the net broken."

No one unfamiliar with the fishermen and the fishing customs of the Lake of Galilee could have written the twenty-first chapter of St. John's Gospel. It happens very often that the man with the hand-net must rely on the advice of someone on shore, who tells him to cast either to the left or right, because in the clear water he can often see a shoal of fish invisible to the man in the water.

Time and again these Galilean fishers are in the habit of casting and getting nothing; but a sudden cast may fall over a shoal and they will be forced to "draw the net to land"— as St. John says so exactly—and their first anxiety is always to discover if the net has been torn.

St. John, in describing the miracle, makes the amazingly matter-of-fact statement that "yet was not the net broken." Who but a fisherman, or one intimately acquainted with them, would dream of mentioning this at such a moment?

The fish we caught were *musht,* or comb-fish. This is the characteristic fish of the Lake of Galilee. It is a flat fish about six inches long, with an enormous head and a comb-like spine that stands up along its back. It is also called St. Peter's Fish, for legend says that it was from the mouth of this fish that Peter took the tribute money.

I sat with a pile of these strange fish before me and remembered the incident as described by St. Matthew. Jesus and Peter had arrived in Capernaum together after the Transfiguration on the slopes of Mount Hermon. One of the gatherers of the Temple Tribute came to demand payment of the half-shekel, levied on every male Jew of religious age. Jesus and Peter were evidently without money, and Jesus said to Peter:

"Go thou to the sea, and cast an hook, and take up the fish that first cometh up; and when thou hast opened his mouth, thou shalt find a piece of money: take that and give unto them for me and thee."

Just out of curiosity I opened the mouth of a *musht* and placed a ten-piaster piece inside it. This is the same size as an English two-shilling piece or about as large as an American half dollar. The coin went in easily, for the mouth of this fish is out of all proportion to its size. The male *musht* has the peculiar habit of carrying the spawn about in his huge mouth, and when the young fish hatch they use the parent's mouth as a nursery and a place of safety in time of danger. As the young fish grow, the mouth of the parent fish becomes so distended that it is difficult to understand how he can feed himself.

But to return to the fishermen. No sooner were the fish dead than one of the men built a little fire of twigs. Another made three slashes with a knife on the backs of the fish and roasted them on the fire. Abdul ran to the boat and brought back with him two or three "loaves," or rather flat cakes of Arab bread, thin, brittle stuff like an overdone pancake.

One of the fish was taken from the fire, placed on a cake of bread and given to me. I pulled it apart with my fingers; and it was very good.

Once again, these fishermen were re-enacting one of the most solemn and beautiful episodes in the Gospel of St.

John. It was in this way—the way the Galilean fishermen always eat when out fishing—that Christ, risen from the grave, commanded the seven disciples to cook the miraculous draught of fishes.

He stood on the shore in the grayness of dawn. At first they did not know Him. When He told them to cast their nets, they obeyed, thinking that He was a fellow fisherman on the bank who had seen a sudden shoal of *musht*. But when they came nearer St. John whispered: "It is the Lord."

"Now when Simon Peter heard that it was the Lord, he girt his fisher's coat unto him (for he was naked) and did cast himself into the sea. And the other disciples came in a little ship; (for they were not far from land, but as it were two hundred cubits) dragging the net with fishes. As soon then as they were come to land, they saw a fire of coals there, and fish laid thereon, and bread. Jesus saith unto them, Bring of the fish which ye have now caught."

I have seen many things in Palestine which have not changed since Bible days, but nowhere else have I met modern men acting quite unconsciously a sacred chapter of the Gospels. The fishermen of Galilee may be Arabs and Moslems, but their habits, their method of work, and the tools of their craft are the same as in the days of Peter, of Andrew and of Philip.

CHAPTER FIVE

I stay in a garden on the shores of the Sea of Galilee. I discover the ruined Church of the Loaves and Fishes. I try to help a dog at Caesarea Philippi.

§ 1

A few miles from Tiberias, and on the same side of the lake, a number of springs well up out of the earth. German Lazarist Fathers have built a little castle there and have set it in an exquisite garden where they love to welcome strangers. The name of this place is Tabgha.

It is as near as possible to the ruins of Capernaum and so I decided to go and live there for a few days. I was given a room overlooking the garden and beyond the trees I could see the lake. I was very happy for that was just as I imagined the Lake of Galilee might be.

When I awakened on the first morning, I felt such an unutterable sense of peace and so great a detachment from the world that I might have been Adam gazing with wonder at the Garden of Eden. My room was set in a tropical jungle of trees. Huge sweet flowers, whose name I do not know, climbed over the little iron balcony and twisted themselves around the windows. Although the sun had only just risen, the blossoms shook with the weight of bees; and down below the blue lake was calm in the first light of the sun. It was so still, so silent, so lovely.

Now I stood in the stillness of the morning looking down on the garden. The sun, rising from behind the Gergesene

Hills, was climbing into the cloudless sky, and the garden was a network of sunlight and shade and full of the little early morning noises, the squeakings, the rustlings, the sound of wings, the cooing of pigeons and, from a fountain buried under trailing flowers, the falling of water.

The years fell shivering away from me and I was at that moment a small boy again, looking out on the lovely world. I seemed to be a part of it and it seemed to be a part of me. The blue kingfisher, balancing himself on the very top of a fir tree, had come to say good morning to me. The little black lizard on the path who, seeing me move, had stopped dead in his tracks with his head lifted also, sharing this moment, shared fellowship. The same joy in life that used to send me running over the meadows at sunrise, that would draw me to the corner of woods where the rabbits played, and to the edge of streams where the trout lay, drove me now to feel and to touch the morning, and hold it in my arms. I flung a towel over my shoulder and went down the garden to a path cut through rocks at the edge of the lake. It ran south into a dark wood of eucalyptus trees that melted into the broad deserted Plain of Gennesaret.

There was not a soul to be seen. At the edge of the wood a stream of fresh water flowed from a pool overhung by precipitous crags. The pool was very still and deep. I flattened myself against a tree trunk and watched two king-fishers diving. They flew in circles over the pool and would suddenly begin to flutter in the air, at the same time point-ing their long beaks toward the water until they looked like poised darts. Then they would drop like stones. They would touch the water swiftly and lightly and rise again; and, as they wheeled, the sun would shine a moment on the

A boy washing the dust from his feet in the pool at the Mosque of
Omar, in Jerusalem.

(Ewing Galloway, N. Y.)

An interesting study in faces as you suffer in a street of modern Jerusalem.

little silver fish in their beaks. The stones were covered with water tortoises. They looked like mud puddings, some dark from the water, others light and sun-dried. When I moved, they slid softly from their rocks into the pool.

The edge of the wood near the lake was a narrow half-moon of shingle. I stepped from my clothes and walked into the Sea of Galilee. The water was painfully cold, but I liked it. The stones underfoot were hard, but I did not mind them. I walked on and on into the shallow water. The sun was warm on my body but my knees were in ice. Soon it was deep enough to swim. I hugged myself in cowardice for a moment and then went in. The water was no longer cold and I struck out toward the Gergesene hills, which rose up from the lake with the morning shadows dark and clear on their sides. I swam back slowly. To the left I could see the shore curving south to Tiberias. I could see the little cluster of white boxes that was the town. In front of me was the green Plain of Gennesaret and the dark belt of the eucalyptus trees. The sensuous, satisfying touch of the water, the beautiful blue water, was ecstasy on this enchanted morning. I heard a clapping in the air and, lying on my back, watched the flock of white pigeons from Tabgha wheeling against the sky. And there was a little silver moon that I had not noticed until then, lying on its back against the blue.

I ran back to Tabgha. And there was honey for breakfast.

§ 2

Five minutes walk from the hospice at Tabgha are the ruins of the Church of the Loaves and Fishes.

No one knows when this church was built. All that is left are the pavement and the stumps of a few pillars. The old Bedouin who guards the precious relic took up a broom and swept away the covering of earth, and with each sweep exquisite little pictures flashed into the sunlight. The floor was formed of small, delicately tinted mosaics in which blue and green predominated. The artist, whoever he was, knew and loved the bird life of the Sea of Galilee and pictured it in a most affectionate way in his little colored stones. The pavement is divided into a number of squares about the size of a large rug, and each square is a design of decorative birds and animals, but so lovingly done, and with a sly sense of humor too, that one can imagine the creator of this pavement hiding in the lake-side reeds, smiling to himself as he watched the often absurd movements of ducks and cranes and the self-assured twittering little birds that hung to the rushes.

I liked his picture of an extraordinarily smug goose pulling a lotus flower. There was another spirited picture, a fight between a heron and a serpent. There were also plump quail. And I admired the astonishing skill he showed in capturing, in what one would imagine to be an intractable material, that sudden moment when a waterfowl stands up in the water and flaps its wings once or twice, like a man yawning and stretching his arms. It is just a flash, and is gone. But this man who centuries ago watched the waterfowl on the Sea of Galilee has managed to pin down this moment in his little tinted stones, for among his triumphs is a bird rather like a crane that is about to flap and stretch, chest out, tail up, and one wing just slightly higher than the other.

The only four-legged animal in the designs of this great but unknown artist is a funny little fellow rather like a rabbit. There is a red ribbon around his neck. I like to think that this was the artist's pet, for a man who observed Nature so accurately and so humorously must have loved animals. I also like to think that he put this little creature into his design in the confident hope that it would please God.

The central theme of the mosaic is a basket containing loaves of bread on each side of which is a fish.

There was something appealing about this pavement because, I suppose, unlike the usual relics of antiquity, a broken pillar or the plinth of a column, it had come out of its grave with a message that conquered time and language. If a voice had suddenly spoken to us from the earth, saying, "I think the wild duck on the lake are very amusing, don't you? Have you noticed how they turn upside down? And have you observed their expressions when they bob up again? Then the fatness of quails and the thinness of storks, how amusing they are!"—if, as I say, a voice had spoken to us in those words, we could not have felt nearer to the artist.

The Miracle of the Feeding of the Five Thousand did not, of course, take place on this side of the lake at all, but the little church must have been a memorial to it.

Standing on the shores of the Sea of Galilee, it is easy to visualize the details of this miracle. News had just been brought to Jesus that Herod Antipas had murdered John the Baptist. He was advised, or perhaps He considered it wise, to withdraw from the territory of Antipas. In order to do so it was necessary only to cross the lake, for the desert mountains of the eastern shore were not in Galilee. Accordingly, says St. Matthew, "he departed thence by ship into a desert place apart." In other words, He crossed over to the deserted eastern banks of the lake.

Now, while the little boat was crossing the six or seven miles of water, a great multitude carrying their sick with them "followed him on foot out of the cities." When you know the shape of the Sea of Galilee, this incident becomes very vivid. Evidently the crowds had converged, as usual, on Capernaum, but when they discovered that the Master had gone, they looked over the water to follow the direction of His boat. They saw with joy that He was going only to the opposite shore, probably to the little fishing port of Bethsaida Julias at the inlet of the Jordan. This meant that if they lost no time and, racing around the northern end of the lake, waded over the shallow Jordan, they would reach Bethsaida Julias almost as soon as Jesus. We can therefore place the Miracle of the Feeding of the Five Thousand more or less accurately as happening on the brown hills nearly opposite Capernaum, for if Jesus had taken a southerly course down the lake the multitudes could not have caught up with Him on foot, and in fact would not have attempted to do so.

As Jesus crossed the water He would see this great race of over five thousand around the north end of the lake, and He would know that whatever thoughts He may have had, of praying in a desert place apart and of meditation on the death of the Forerunner, were fated to be given up in service to the crowds. No sooner had He landed than the crowds came to Him, and we learn that He "was moved with compassion toward them, because they were as sheep not having a shepherd."

With the approach of sunset and the swift coming of night the disciples became anxious for the multitude, hungry and in a desert place. They advised Jesus to disband them and send them home.

"Give ye them to eat," answered Jesus.

They returned to say that only five loaves and two fishes could be found. St. John, whose account of the miracle is remarkable and detailed, says that the loaves and fishes belonged to a boy. The exact words are: "There is a lad here, which hath five barley loaves, and two small fishes: but what are they among so many?"

Commentators have imagined that this lad was one of the bread boys who are still to be seen in Arab towns, sometimes with strips of dried fish which they sell with the bread.

"And Jesus took the loaves; and when he had given thanks, he distributed to the disciples, and the disciples to them that were set down; and likewise of the fishes as much as they would. When they were filled, he said unto his disciples, gather up the fragments that remain, that nothing be lost."

There is one point in St. John's account of the miracle which is extremely interesting. In describing the fish eaten on this occasion he uses the Greek word *opsarion*, which our translators render as "small fish." St. John is the only evangelist to use this word, and the real meaning is not "small fish" but "a savory dish" or, as we might say, hors d'œuvres. This is exactly what the small pickled fish of Galilee were in the time of Christ.

This is a wonderful instance of the vivid local color which has been detected in the Fourth Gospel, because no one unacquainted with the life and speech of Galilee could have employed this word.

Again, so it seems to me, St. John conclusively proves his Galilean origin in his account of our Lord's appearance to the disciples in the dawn, when they are fishing near the shore. Who except a fisherman would have worried about the condition of his net at such a moment? The Master who had been crucified was standing in the grayness of the dawn, calling to them from the shore, but St. John says that when they drew the great haul of fish to land "yet was not the net broken."

It would never occur to a man of any other occupation, and certainly never to a student writing in a study, to note such a detail. But the Galilean fisherman who nets a heavy catch is always anxious about the net, because the bottom of the lake is covered with sharp stones for perhaps twenty or thirty feet before the sand begins. What a shouting goes up today as a heavy net is drawn out of the deep water toward the sharp stones; with what care the fishermen run thigh-deep into the lake to lift the precious burden clear of rocks!

In revealing details like this, and in the use of the word *opsarion,* St. John proclaims his origin.

§ 3

I awakened at sunrise and went down to the lake side.

I was surprised to see at that early hour a little black dot which was a rowboat in the center of the lake. Suddenly I heard through the still morning air a remarkable sound. It was the noise of a typewriter.

134 ·

I can conceive no time and place where the sound of a typewriter is more surprising than at sunrise on the Sea of Galilee. The boat was too far from land for me to distinguish those inside it, and it went off, keeping well in the middle of the lake, toward Magdala. But there was no mistaking that familiar tap, tap-tap, tap-tap-tap-tap over the stillness of the morning sea.

I went back up the stone water steps into the garden, and while I was dressing I began to worry about the typewriter. It seemed too improbable. Could I have been mistaken? For a moment I wondered whether the sun had affected me. Many people are suddenly knocked out by sunstroke in Palestine. I began to think of the sound of that tap-tapping with an almost superstitious fear. An ordinary typewriter is bad enough, but the idea of a supernatural typewriter makes the blood run cold.

Later in the morning, when I was writing on the little balcony that ran around my room, I heard it again. A typewriter! It was loud and fluent. I leaped up and ran to the railings. Down below me, sitting at a little table which he had brought out from the lounge, was a tall, thin, middle-aged man. He was dressed in a gray tweed suit and, although it was blazing hot, he had made no concessions: he was wearing a stiff white collar and a buttoned-up coat. His fingers traveled rapidly over the keys and he was intent and lost in the web of his words.

Pausing a moment for a word, he caught sight of my fascinated face on the balcony.

"I hope I'm not disturbing you," he said, "if I am, I'll..."

"On the contrary, you've relieved my mind."

He gave me a shy smile.

· 135

"May I ask if you are writing a book?" I said.

"Oh no," he replied, and gave a deprecating little laugh. "Nothing like that. I'm writing to my wife."

One learns never to be surprised when one travels, but this man did surprise me.

"Were you writing to your wife," I asked, "as the sun was rising this morning?"

"Oh, you saw me?"

"No, I heard you, quite clearly."

"Yes, it was all part of the same letter," he said.

"If it won't interrupt you too much, I'd like to come down and talk to you."

He gave me a friendly smile, and I ran down the stairs and went over to him. He was, as I say, tall and thin, with a white mustache and spectacles. There was a pile of typed manuscript on his little table, about five thousand words. He saw me glance at it, fascinated.

"That's my next letter," he said. "I shall post it when I get back to Jerusalem."

And they say that the age of letter writing is dead!

"You see," he explained, "I come from Australia. All my life I have longed to travel. All my life! And my wife has let me take a trip around the world. I shall be away nearly a year. So, you see, I feel that the least I can do is to write to her every day. But I like to write to her when I'm actually doing something, if you see what I mean, so that she can feel that she is with me. For instance, I wrote her a letter from the top of the Great Pyramid when I was in Egypt. I typed her another from the top of the Leaning Tower of Pisa. It makes it more vivid and real."

He took up a page of typescript:

136 .

"Now this morning I begin, 'I am writing to you from a boat on the Sea of Galilee, and it is nearly five A.M. The sun has just risen and we are rowing slowly along' . . . you see the idea?"

My first feeling of amusement melted into a warmth of friendliness for him. His disarming smile and his tremendous enthusiasm were attractive and unusual in a man of his age.

"It's hot out here," he said. "Would you like to come to my room and have a chat? I love talking to people. It gives me more to write about, too."

He led the way under the hibiscus-covered archway near the little chapel. A bed had been made up for him in a kind of ground-floor vault known as "the museum." His shaving stick and razor were standing among fragments from the excavation of the Church of the Loaves and Fishes. His suitcase was propped up on a couple of broken Roman columns, and he could not unpack because of the litter of Roman and Greek glass and pottery, coins, handles of amphoræ and fragments of Byzantine mosaic by which he was surrounded.

"Rather unique!" he smiled.

"Tell me," I said, "are you disappointed in travel? Is the world as wonderful as you thought it would be?"

"I know what you mean," he said, looking grave. "No; I'm not disappointed. I think the world is wonderful."

Again he gave me that charming, shy smile.

"I think you're rather wonderful," I told him, "because you have set out in middle age with all the fire of youth in you. If I might make a frightful pun, you seen to have escaped the hardening of the hearteries."

"Well, it's just the way one looks at things. . . . But I've had some wonderful experiences. Would it bore you? I have! Wonderful! I was received by the Pope. There were a lot of other people there, too, of course! I don't want you to think that His Holiness saw me alone, or anything like that. I knelt there with my hand full of rosaries and as he passed he blessed them, and, although I'm a Protestant and teach in Sunday school, I said, as he passed, 'God bless you' —just like that! And do you know why I said it? So that I could write and tell my wife that I had spoken to the Pope."

A gleam of happiness and triumph came into his eyes.

"I make it a point," he went on, "of swimming in every famous river and lake. I have swum in the Thames, the Seine, the Moskva at Moscow, the Tiber, the Abana at Damascus, and in the Dead Sea and the Sea of Galilee. I nearly got arrested in Rome for swimming in the Tiber. The current is very strong, but I only went in and out, just long enough to fill my bottle."

"I don't understand."

"You see, I am taking back with me to Australia little bottles containing the waters of all the famous rivers and lakes. They'll think a lot of them at home. Here they are in my suitcase. Looks like a chemist's shop, doesn't it? And those stones. Do you know where they came from? From the river bed where David slew Goliath."

We talked on into the hot afternoon, or rather he talked and I sat admiring his zest for life. Everything was, to him, exciting and superlative. "I am always ready for adventures," he said. Genuine enthusiasm carries with it an entirely spurious atmosphere of originality. Yet is that true? The man was really blazing a trail through all the well-

138 .

worn paths of the world: he was blazing it through the terrific jungle of his own enthusiasm. I admired him because he was so genuinely in love with the world. He had absolutely no shred of cynicism.

"There's one thing I would appreciate," he said. "I'd love you to take a photograph of me bathing in the Sea of Galilee."

"I'll do it with pleasure."

"Well, let me find my bathing suit. Here we are and—here's my camera!"

He strode off into the blazing sun, bareheaded, but with his tweed coat still buttoned. He undressed behind a clump of eucalyptus trees, and when he was reclining in the Sea of Galilee, with the happy expression of a boy of ten, I waded in and snapped the shutter.

"Thank you," he said. "That will be immensely appreciated at home! Are you sure you've wound the film?"

§ 4

In the time of Jesus the Sea of Galilee was one of the busiest centers of life in the country, and the western shore was ringed with towns and villages. The ruler of the province had his palace on the hill above Tiberias. The lake was crowded with ships.

One has always imagined that Jesus preached His Gospel to simple country folk in a remote part of Palestine where no whisper of the outside world ever interrupted the immortal current of His thought. In actual fact His Ministry was conducted not only in the most cosmopolitan region in the country, but also in a territory where the ancient trade

routes from Tyre and Sidon on the west, and the old caravan roads from Damascus on the northeast, as well as the
great imperial highways, met together and branched out
over the country. Galilee was on the main road of the ancient world, a halfway house between Damascus and the
Egyptian frontier, on one hand, and between Antioch and
Jerusalem on the other.

It was also a busy agricultural and industrial district.
The hills around the lake, now so desolate, were planted
with palms, olives, figs and vines. The fruits grown around
the Sea of Galilee were famous in Biblical times. The
trades carried on around the lake were boat-building, dye-
ing (at Magdala), pottery works and fish curing. The large
curing factory was at Tarichaea—the "pickling place"—to
the south of the lake, where fish were salted and packed for
export.

In attempting to reconstruct the busy life of the Sea of
Galilee as Jesus saw it, we must also remember that the
hills, now so bare, were at that time covered with trees. An
intricate system of aqueducts, whose ruins are to be seen
here and there (notably in some rocks at the back of the
hospice at Tabgha), carried streams of fresh water wherever
they are required. The climate must have been less fever-
ridden than it is today. Possibly the wooded hills attracted
a greater rainfall and also tempered the heat. One must
think of this beautiful blue lake barred by a rampart of
brown barren hills to the east, and ringed on the western
shore with an almost unbroken chain of little towns lying
at the foot of green hills thick with woods, bright with gardens, and loud with the music of running water. There
would be the docks and harbor of Tarichaea, the long

rows of sheds, the sound of hammers as the coopers barreled the fish, the noise of shipbuilders—possibly at Capernaum —the smoke and smell of the dye works at Magdala, and the pottery kilns. On the hill behind the regal city of Tiberias rose the magnificent Herodian palace whose Greek sculptures shone in the sun from afar: well-built town walls met the lake water and enclosed streets, villas, theaters and an amphitheater where Greeks, Romans and Sadducees applauded touring companies from Antioch, or watched gladiators whose names were famous throughout the Decapolis.

The lake as Jesus knew it must have been one of the busiest and most cosmopolitan districts of Palestine. Greek, Latin, and Aramaic were spoken in its towns. Its people were immersed in the affairs of the moment, and were, in fact, a part of that vivid, variegated world balanced between the East and the West: the world of the Gospels and the Early Church.

When Jesus walked the roads of Galilee He met the long caravans working southward across the fords of Jordan; He saw the sun gleam on the spears of Roman maniples and cohorts; He met bands of Phoenecian merchants traveling into Galilee; encountered the litters and chariots of the great, and saw the bands of strolling players and jugglers and gladiators bound for the gay Greek cities of the Decapolis.

The shadow of this world falls across the pages of the New Testament. Jesus, walking the roads of Galilee, is walking the modern world, with its money-changers and its tax-collectors, its market places and its unhappy rich men. When we think of Him beside the Sea of Galilee, we must

· 141

not imagine Him as retired from the world, preaching His Gospel to a few faithful, simple souls: we must realize that He had chosen to live among people of many nations and upon one of the main highways of the Roman Empire.

§ 5

I took the boat one morning and rowed among the lonely little bays to the north of Tabgha. It was a perfect day and I had not seen the lake a deeper blue. The bare hills rose from the water to lie in gentle curves against the sky. Piles of black basalt lay everywhere, on the hills and at the water's edge, and so characteristic is this volcanic stone that even the lizards have colored themselves in imitation of it. In the curve of a small bay a white temple hides itself among hedges and eucalyptus trees. There are four columns upholding a broken architrave, a paved court in which the grass grows, a doorway that leads nowhere, and the usual chaos of broken pillars and fallen stones. Most scholars now agree that this is all that is left of Capernaum.

I tied up the boat and, walking through the garden of the Franciscan friars, who have their dwelling near by, wandered among the tumbled stones. The temple is the ruin of Capernaum's synagogue. Some experts say that it is the very building in which Jesus preached and performed His miracles; others say that it is not actually the building, but one erected much later on the same spot. But does it matter? It was here that Jesus Christ lived during the two or three most important years in the world's history. Somewhere among the piles of black basalt that scatter the hillocks is the site of Peter's house, where our Lord lived; somewhere on the little curve of shore is the very spot where "he saw Simon and Andrew, his brother, casting a net into the sea: for they were fishers. And Jesus said unto them, 'Come ye after me and I will make you to become fishers of men.' " A little farther along the shore is the place where James and John, the sons of Zebedee, left their father in the boat with the hired servants in order to follow the Master. Perhaps on this very spot, deserted now except by the little black lizards that run among the stones, Jesus expelled the unclean spirit and healed the man with a withered hand. If not from this bay, from one exactly like it, Jesus put out in a little boat and spoke to the multitudes that were gathered on the shore.

This white ruin amid the eucalyptus grove is, I think, one of the most touching links with our Lord's Ministry to be seen in the Holy Land. The Franciscan friars, who guard each stone with love and reverence, have left untouched this white ruin facing the lake, so that one can sit there and know that Jesus, when He stood there, looked across the blue water to the parched hills of "the desert place" opposite, and saw, to the south, the lake stretching into a heat haze that gives an illusion of the sea.

One sits in the ruin of this building watching the blue lake, trying hard to build up a picture of Jesus as He appeared to His contemporaries. What did He look like and how was He dressed? The traditional, bareheaded Jesus of Christian art cannot be correct. Perhaps Dr. Stapfer has drawn a more authentic portrait in his *Palestine in the Time of Christ:*

· 143

"He had neither the fine linen nor the sumptuous raiment of those who live in kings' houses," he wrote, "neither had he a long flowing robe like the scribes and Pharisees. Upon His head He must have worn the turban, the national headgear, used alike by rich and poor. Painters make a mistake when they represent Christ bareheaded. As we have said, everyone wore the head covered. The turban He wore was probably white. It was fastened under the chin by a cord, and at the side fell down to the shoulders and over the tunic. Under His turban He wore his hair rather long and His beard uncut. His tunic, and underneath vesture, was of one piece without seam; it was therefore of some value (John xix. 23) and had probably been given Him by one of those women who 'ministered to Him of their substance.' Over this He wore the *talith,* loose and flowing. The mantle was not white, for we are told it became white during the Transfiguration. It was not red, for that was only the military color. It is possible it was blue, for blue was then very common, or it may have been simply white with brown stripes. In any case, Jesus had at the four corners of this mantle the *Ciccith,* the blue or white fringes of which we have just spoken. He wore sandals on His feet, as we learn from John the Baptist; and when He was traveling, going from place to place, He doubtless wore a girdle round the loins and carried a stick in His hand. . . ."

I rowed back toward Tabgha and came ashore at the place where probably Capernaum ended. Here are several huge heart-shaped stones called the *Mensa Christi,* and they were in all probability the quayside stones of the ancient town.

If these stones are really the ancient quayside of Capernaum, they are one of the most interesting relics in Palestine. May it not have been on the quayside that St. Matthew was sitting at the receipt of custom? Until I came to Palestine I imagined that St. Matthew was stationed at a customhouse on the extreme northern limit of the lake, probably a kind of frontier between Galilee and Gaulonitis. But, reading the Gospels on the spot, one cannot help thinking that St. Matthew was not on the road but on the lake side. "And he went forth again by the seaside: and all the multitude resorted unto him, and he taught them. And as he passed by, he saw Levi the son of Alphæus sitting at the receipt of custom, and said unto him, Follow me. And he arose and followed him." It would seem clear from St. Mark that the customhouse was near the lake. If so, it was for the purpose of taking a tax on goods landed and a percentage of fish caught by the fishermen. The only place for such a tollhouse would have been on the landing stage.

Matthew was obviously only one of many detested publicans around the Sea of Galilee. The place must have swarmed with them. It was a frontier district, and everything coming into it from the many caravan roads, from the neighboring tetrarchy of Philip, or from the opposite side of the lake which was Greek territory, was subject to duty. Herod's income from his tetrarchy was two hundred talents (about $130,000), and we may be sure that the publicans squeezed out the last cent.

Matthew, who is often spoken of as a Roman official, was really nothing of the kind. He was a local *douanier* in the employment of Herod Antipas. The Talmud mentions two kinds of publicans: the general taxgatherer *(Gabbai)* and the customhouse official *(Mokhes,* or *Mokhsa),* both of whom were as heartily loathed and detested by Jews in the time of Christ as the landlord's agent was detested in nineteenth-century Ireland. In Judea the taxgatherer was the minion of an oppressive alien administration, in Galilee he was the agent of an equally greedy autocrat.

One imagines that Matthew, if his post was on the quayside at Capernaum, had many an opportunity of seeing Jesus as he arrived or departed. This is the opinion of Dr. Edersheim, who paints a beautiful little picture in *The Life and Times of Jesus the Messiah:*

"We take it, long before that eventful day that for ever decided his life, Matthew had, in heart, become a disciple of Jesus. Only he dared not, could not, have hoped for personal recognition—far less for call to discipleship. But when it came, and Jesus fixed on him that look of love which searched the inmost deep of the soul, and made Him the true Fisher of men, it needed not a moment's thought or consideration. When he spake it, 'Follow Me,' the past seemed all swallowed up in the present heaven of bliss. He said not a word, for his soul was in the speechless surprise of unexpected love and grace; but he rose up, left the customhouse, and followed Him."

The most solemn and wonderful association of these strange heart-shaped stones is that of the gray dawn over the lake side, when Jesus appeared to seven of the disciples after the Resurrection. They did not recognize Him. They saw a lonely figure standing on the shore and they heard a voice calling to them. If these stones are what tradition claims them to be, it was upon them that the Risen Christ prepared "a fire of coals" and "fish laid thereon, and bread." As the gray light brightened into sunrise, one of the most moving incidents in the Gospels took place when Peter was forgiven for his denial and was bidden, as in the first days of his discipleship, to "Follow me."

And it was from these stones that the little band of followers heard the words which sum up the whole duty of the pastoral office:

"Feed my lambs."

§ 6

Throughout the month of March the cranes fly north over the Sea of Galilee. They migrate from Central Africa and journey up through Palestine to Russia. "The stork in the heaven knoweth her appointed times; and the turtle and the crane and the swallow observe the time of their coming: but my people know not the judgement of the Lord," said Jeremiah.

I shall always think of the flight of the cranes as one of the most characteristic sights of Galilee. They fly at a great height and you might not notice them until the sun, shining on their white feathers, turns them into a snowstorm against the blue sky. They move slowly, wheeling in the air, in great companies many thousands strong, sometimes seeming to stop and wheel above one particular spot as though contemplating a descent. But in half an hour, if you look for them again, they have vanished against the white head of Mount Hermon.

Everywhere around Tabgha you see black and white kingfishers, generally in pairs. They hover above the Sea of Galilee like hawks and plunge down to the water, rarely failing to rise with a small fish. These white and black kingfishers, so plain in plumage compared with the iridescent blue-green kingfishers of English streams or the flashing blue American species, remind me of a curious legend about this bird. The story goes that they were all originally gray or white and received their lovely colors when, released from the Ark, they flew straight into the light of a sunset. How the kingfishers of Galilee escaped the Flood I am not prepared to say!

There are several other birds very like our own brilliant kingfishers, but these are the Smyrna ice-birds and the bee-eaters.

The most homely sound on the Sea of Galilee is the chirping of sparrows. There is a tremendous colony of them in the eucalyptus wood at Tabgha and every evening they set up a shrill chirping that lasts until dusk, when they settle down and go to sleep.

This grove is the most exquisite spot on the Sea of Galilee. It is always cool under the tall trees, and the ground underfoot is soft and crackling with dead leaves, almost like a wood at home.

I can sit there for hours in the heat of the day, watching the kingfishers and the water tortoises. The tortoises are very timid, but the young and inexperienced sometimes lie on the edge of the stream instead of occupying stones in the center. It is easy to catch them, and you are rewarded by the sight of a funny little snake's head popping back into its shell and the beady glance of two sharp slanting black eyes. They swim with remarkable speed under water, and you can trace their journeys by the blunt noses thrust above the surface every so often as they come up for air.

The Lake of Galilee is, of all the places that I have seen, the one in which the Spirit of Christ is still present. There are no warring sects, no rival shrines; only lake water falling on black stones, a slow procession of crops, the ripening of fruit, the bright flight of kingfisher and bee-catcher, the sun by day and the stars by night.

Time has taken no revenge on the lake side where Christianity was born. It is even lovelier than imagination paints it. There are no temples made by hands, no clash of creed, no jealousy and no hate.

In the silence of night the little fishing boats set off under the stars as they used to do when a Voice called from the shore: "Come ye after me, and I will make you fishers of men."

§ 7

To the north of Galilee the mountains lift their heads into the sky and the tallest of these is Mount Hermon, where the snow sometimes lasts through the hot summer. It was to the slopes of these mountains near the town of Caesarea Philippi, that Jesus retired with his disciples and told them of his approaching crucifixion.

I wanted to see what is left of this ancient city and so one morning I hired a car and drove for some hours into the deserted foothills. I came at last to a miserable and dirty little Arab village, which is all that is left of the once brilliant and beautiful Caesarea Philippi. Long before the time of Christ the place was called Panias because it contained a dark cave which was sacred to the god Pan, and, strange to say, the old name has come back, but because there is no *p* in the Arabic alphabet it is called Banias.

A ruined city is a sad sight, and when you see the ends of marble columns and the fragments of carved ceilings and of statues built into the walls of cow sheds and outhouses, it is sadder still. I looked around me, unable to believe that a beautiful city had ever stood there. But I found that the mysterious cave of Pan still exists, overgrown with trees and choked with stones and rubbish. An Arab took me there and in the darkness I heard a queer stirring as of something alive. It was water welling up in the cave, which is one of the sources of the river Jordan. It is easy to understand why the Arabs believe the cave to be haunted. The Arab told me that only the night before the whole village had been awakened by a voice calling to prayer.

"It was a prophet," he said in explanation.

The Moslem believes that while the souls of ordinary men wait for the resurrection, the souls of prophets can move about and make themselves heard and seen. He told me that someone in the village had caught sight of the spirit, and that he "was very white and not like an Arab."

As I walked from the grotto into the poor little village of Banias, I saw something lying in the road that at first I took to be an old coat, or a garment that someone had thrown away. Then it moved, and I saw that it was a dog. I thought that it had been run over and went closer to it. The poor thing was a Saluki dying of hunger.

She was so weak that she could not move. She could only lie in the hot dust of the road, too weak to shake the flies from her sores. Her eyes were lost in a world of unutterable pain. She was grotesque and misshapen with suffering. Her ears had been clipped close to her head—a common habit with the Bedouin, who believe that to clip the ears of a dog increases its hearing.

I had never in my life seen an animal in such a ghastly condition. She was too weak to run away from me. She lay in the road, watching with her pitiful eyes and waiting for me to hurt her.

When I brought sandwiches from the car and tried to feed her with small pieces of meat, she could not realize that I was attempting to help her. She looked frightened. Then, very gently, she took a piece of meat in her parched, scarred mouth, but it fell out into the dust.

I found myself blazing with anger. The utter callousness of the Mohammedan for the suffering of animals is a terrible thing. Two or three Arabs gathered around and watched me as if I were a lunatic; as, indeed, they thought I was.

"She dies of hunger," they said.

"Why does nobody feed her?" I asked.

"She belongs to nobody," they replied. "The Bedouin left her. She does not belong to this place."

That was their point of view. She belonged to no one. Allah had **given** her life. Let Allah take away the life he had given. It was not their affair. So, after stoning her for a bit, they had permitted her to lie about and die.

She managed to eat two or three pieces of meat. She lay

in the hot dust, begging me with her terrible eyes not to leave her.

"Has anyone got a gun?" I asked.

They looked shifty and lied. "No," they said.

"Well, a knife?"

Yes, they had knives. I offered two dollars to any of them who would put the poor thing out of her pain; but, although two dollars would have been more than three months' income to any of them, they looked at me with horror and flatly refused. The dog must die when Allah willed.

I found two Armenian policemen in the village, but they refused to do anything. They knew the dog and would very much like to shoot her, but it would cause trouble in the village. These people were very devout Moslems. They were afraid nothing could be done. They were sorry and sympathetic. They brought out tins of black tobacco and, shrugging their shoulders, rolled themselves cigarettes.

The greater the opposition the more I was determined to help the dog, even if it meant sleeping among the fleas of Banias for a week. There were three things to do: kill her myself, which I dreaded because of her eyes; to take her away in the car, but she was mangy, unable to move, and would certainly be refused by any hotel; or to find someone who would swear to take care of her. This I eventually did. He was a nice, gentle Arab in an old suit of khaki. I was told that his job was to sweep out the shrine at El Kedir.

I gave him money to buy food for the animal, and warned him that I would return within a week to see how she was getting on. He looked at me as though he knew that, although quite mad, I was serious. I made him pick up the dog and show me where he was going to keep her. He led the way, followed now by the entire village, to his house. This was a desperately poor little hovel enclosed by a high mud wall. There was a yard with several one-story houses opening onto it.

He placed the dog tenderly in the shade and brought a few sacks for her to lie on. A woman came out of a house and watched the proceedings with a complete absence of feeling, although the animal's plight was enough to have wrung a word of sympathy from a fiend. I felt that I had done all that I could do and, warning the man that I would return, I went away.

As I traveled on I began to wonder whether I had done the right thing. It was almost cruel to attempt to revive the pale spark of life in a creature so near to death.

I traveled for hours through a smiling land of hills and valleys. I saw a crusader's castle perched like an eagle's aerie on the crest of a mountain. And far off I saw the blue Mediterranean and the road that runs to Sidon.

§ 8

In about a week's time I determined to go back and see what had happened to the dog. I got to Banias before noon rather angry and impatient but these feelings were immediately swept aside as soon as I entered the village.

I should have realized that I had been the sole topic of conversation in Caesarea Philippi for a whole week! I should have known that those who were at work on the mountainside were told about me when they came home; that some who had never seen me gave long and vivid accounts of the incredibly mad stranger who had stayed to pick a dog out of the road. The result was that as soon as I appeared the whole village gathered around, but not with the grim, hard expression which terrifies nervous tourists: they were all laughing and smiling, and a cry went up *"Abu kelb, Abu kelb!"* which means "Father of the dog."

The Arab is a great hand shaker. I went around the group shaking hands, telling the driver to ask them how the dog was.

"Come and see, O *Abu Kelb!*" was the reply.

And a crowd of bare-legged little children went running up between the mud walls announcing the great and spectacular news that *"Abu kelb,* the father of the dog," had returned.

I was led to the squalid little hovel behind the mud walls. The crowd was so great that we had to shut the gate, but the children climbed up on the wall to watch. A white mare was tethered in the yard. A *douanier,* whom I had not seen before, came out of the house, dressed in a pair of khaki breeches and a gray army shirt. He shook me warmly by the hand, explaining in French that he was a lodger in the house, but had unfortunately been out on duty when I had been there before. His name was John. Now, however, how happy he was to make my acquaintance! How glad he was that I had come back. Two little boys brought wooden stools from a house and set them in the shade. The *douanier* sat on one and I sat on the other. The women and children grouped themselves around us. All the time the *douanier* bubbled with affability and I gazed around for the dog, but could not see her. My heart sank. So she was dead! Perhaps it was just as well. But I was too familiar with the habits of the Arabs to ask any questions. All would be known in time.

The *douanier,* it appeared, was an Armenian from Aleppo. He had a great affection for England. He had learned English from a priest at a mission school in Aleppo. Ah, if some day he could go to London! He would like that very much. The English were a great nation. The last war was a sad affair. All wars are sad. All the English love dogs. The Arabs do not love dogs. But he, an Armenian from Aleppo, he loved dogs like the English. So he rattled on. Then the crowd parted and the man who sweeps out the shrine of El Kedir came up with the Saluki.

I could hardly believe my eyes. She could stand! Her hind legs trembled woefully and her tail, bare and mangy, was still well down. But her eyes had lost the fear of death, although they were still full of pain.

The Arab had made her a little coat from a pair of khaki trousers and he had bound up the wounds on her forelegs with pieces of rag. The Armenian explained that he had bathed her wounds with wine and oil—the remedy which the Good Samaritan used on the wounded traveler.

The dog seemed to know in some way that I was the cause of her present well-being and she did something which completely finished me. She walked up to me and just rested her bruised muzzle on my knee. I decided at that moment that, grotesque and blown out with starvation as she was, wounded, mangy and sore, I would somehow take her home with me to England.

I thought how extraordinary it is that a show of interest and a little money can make so much difference to any living thing. The poor creature that a week ago had been

stoned and kicked about was now a feature of the village.
She was the protégé of the rich, mad Englishman.

I asked the Armenian what would happen if I did not
take her away.

"This man," he replied, pointing to the Arab, "will look
after her as long as you pay, but when you stop paying he
will turn her loose, because he is too poor to buy food for
her."

I told him of my intention of taking the dog to Jerusalem. He shook his head. The Palestine Customs would
not allow her to enter in her present condition. But if I got
an order from the government? I suggested. Yes, it might
be done.

So we agreed that they should continue the feeding and
the bathing of the dog, and I handed out some more *baksheesh*.

"That is the name of the dog," I explained. "I shall call
her 'Baksheesh.' "

This was a joke that everybody understood!

I went off, promising that I would either call again at
Banias or send someone in my name to take "Baksheesh"
into Palestine. And as I went off I heard the children shouting *"Abu kelb!"*

Weeks later I got a letter which read:

"My dear friend, Mr. Morton, I am verry glade I
get a great satisfaction by this relation which com-
menced with a dog. You can be able for its hospitality.
I brought a big jar of sea water from Sidon by which
I wash it evry day, morning and evening. Now it is

156 .

better than bifore. I hope that we will not forget ourselves, and I am allways redy to execute your commis-
sions. Excuse me for my mistakes, because the last war
of Turkey in 1920 which resulted after two years with
all Christchen immegration has destroyed our futur
and high life. God be with you till we meet.

JOHN."

It was from the excellent Customs Officer at Banias. So
he was bathing the dog with water from Sidon.

That sounded excellent.

In a few days I was able, through the kindness of the
Palestine Government, to get poor "Baksheesh" through the
Customs and into the kennels of the S.P.C.A. in Jerusalem,
an organization that, although dying for lack of money, is
striving hard to make the Arab understand that animals can
feel and suffer.

The report was encouraging. I saw myself taking "Baksheesh" for walks in Hyde Park and for long tramps over the
Sussex Downs. Then one day I received a letter saying that
she was dead. She was too weak to stand treatment.

"Knowing how much you cared," wrote Mrs. Reynolds, a
member of the Society, "I have buried her in my own garden, where you can think of her sleeping among the rock
flowers."

When I was near Banias again I made a detour to thank
John for all his kindness. The Arabs and the children
crowded around my car with cries of "*Abu kelb!*" looking
and peering into the car for "Baksheesh." I told them she
was dead.

"It is the will of Allah!" they said.

And they looked at me with the respectful sympathy due to any man who tries to defy the inscrutable will of God. Even John, the Good Samaritan, said it was a good thing, and that when I went to Aleppo he would give me two much finer dogs. Even he did not understand that the crucified eyes of poor "Baksheesh" had marked her out from all the other dogs upon this earth.

CHAPTER SIX

I go to Jerusalem for Easter, I attend the ceremonies of the Washing of the Feet, the Holy Fire and the Searching for the Body of Christ. In the exciting atmosphere of the Holy City I attempt to reconstruct the events which led to the Crucifixion.

§ 1

As Easter was approaching I hurried back to Jerusalem in order to see the many strange and ancient ceremonies of Holy Week.

Jerusalem was filled with the people of all nations. I heard French, German, Italian, English, Arabic, Yiddish and Hebrew in the course of one short walk through the streets. Droves of superior tourists had come to gaze curiously on the rites of the Eastern Church and were queerly mixed with humble Eastern Christians who firmly believed that the Holy Fire was soon to descend from heaven upon the Tomb of Christ. Rich Jews from far away had come to eat the Passover in the City of David and Solomon. The Moslems were talking of the great pilgrimage to the tomb of Moses near Jericho.

The little shops near the Holy Sepulcher overflowed with incense and became festooned with the richest of candles. Large piles of shrouds appeared outside them on chairs. They were of the thinnest, cheapest linen and bore, printed in black, rough pictures of the Passion. I saw a peasant woman from, I think, Bulgaria, buy a shroud. Although they were all the same, she went from shop to shop examining them and fingering the miserable texture. It must have been force of habit.

In the dimness of Calvary a forest of candles burned; and all day long silent crowds knelt before the Tomb of Christ. In the dark streets of the old city the Jews watched the moon of Nisan grow full, and went about their intricate preparations with an air of furtive secrecy; for the Passover was near.

I had been invited to a house on the outskirts of Jerusalem to eat the Passover with a Jewish family. I was late because I had been given an insufficient address and wandered lost for some time in a solitude like that of Christmas night. The streets were deserted. I could hear cheerful festal sounds from the front rooms of houses, and once, through a badly drawn curtain, I saw a number of people sitting round a brilliantly lit table, the men with their caps on.

The moonlight was a green rain falling on everything. The shadows had a depth and softness that was exquisite to see, and on a piece of broken ground where someone was building a house I came across a solitary olive tree shining in the moonlight among piles of bricks and stones, its little leaves silvered all over as if covered with frost.

At last I found the house and was delighted to discover that I had not kept my hosts waiting. I was given a skull-cap and we went into the dining room, where the grandfather of the assembly took his seat at the head of the table. He explained the setting of the table to me: the shankbone of lamb, the relic of the Paschal sacrifice; the roasted egg, symbolic of the daily Temple offering; the plate of *haro-*

Narrow, cobbled street steps in Jerusalem.

(A. F. Kersting)

View from the path outside the city wall on the east side of Jerusalem.

seth, made of apples, almonds, raisins, chopped cinnamon and wine, said to represent the clay from which the children of Israel made bricks; the bitter herbs and the dish of vinegar, symbolic of the years of bondage in Egypt. An extra cup of wine stood on the table. This was called "the cup of Elijah." In Jewish tradition the prophet is a wandering angel who may enter any house unbidden on the night of the Passover.

The head of the house, reclining easily against a great pile of cushions, looked round on his children and grandchildren and began the ceremony that celebrates the escape of Israel from Egypt. All over the world this strange race, which has retained its sense of difference throughout the centuries, was performing exactly the same ceremony.

The sanctification, or *Kiddush,* was pronounced, after which we solemnly drank a glass of red wine and water. A maidservant came round with a bowl and a jug. She poured water over our hands. Parsley dipped in vinegar was distributed. The head of the household broke the middle *matzah* cake on the dish before him and concealed half of it, leaving the other half covered with a napkin.

These words came into my mind: "And as they did eat, Jesus took bread, and blessed, and brake it, and gave to them, and said, Take eat: this is my body."

Shining from the solemn ordinance of the Old Testament was the Holy Eucharist that on this night nineteen centuries ago, and within a mile of the place where we were sitting, had been instituted by the Priest who was also the Sacrifice.

The people at the table began to whisper together, asking

who was the youngest. Presently a girl of about twenty stood up and asked her grandfather:

"Why is this night distinguished from all other nights?"

Then the old man repeated the ancient story of the Passover that has been kept green in the memory of Israel, and of the Jews, since Moses led the way out of Egypt. When he had ended, the first of the *Hallel* Psalms was sung:

"Blessed art Thou, O Eternal! who redeemeth Israel," chanted the master of the house. "Blessed art Thou, O Eternal, our God! King of the Universe, Creator of the fruit of the vine."

We lifted our glasses and drank the second cup of wine.

"Verily I say unto you," said Christ at the Last Supper, "I will drink no more of the fruit of the vine, until that day that I drink it new in the kingdom of God."

Once more water was poured over our hands and the host gave to each of us a piece of the broken unleavened bread, which we ate with this blessing:

"Blessed art Thou, O Eternal, our God, King of the Universe, who bringeth forth bread from the earth. Blessed art Thou, O Eternal, our God, King of the Universe, who hath sanctified us with Thy commandments, and commanded us to eat unleavened bread."

The host next took the bitter herbs, the green tops of horseradish, and after dipping them in the *haroseth* gave some to each guest.

Again we ate unleavened bread, but this time with bitter herbs. Then followed an excellent dinner. At the end of it the host took the broken *matzah* cake and handed a small portion—called the *aficoman*—to each guest. He said grace and we drank the third cup of wine. The door of the house was flung open with this defiant appeal to God:

"Pour out Thy wrath upon the heathen that know Thee not, and upon the kingdoms that call not upon Thy name. They have devoured Jacob and laid waste his dwelling place. Pour out upon them Thine indignation and let Thy wrathful anger overtake them. Pursue them in anger, and destroy them from under the heavens of the Lord."

The fourth cup of wine was then filled and, after the singing of the *Hallel,* was emptied.

I said good night to the kindly folk who had admitted me, a stranger and a Gentile, to this intimate glimpse of an ancient faith, and walked out again into the moonlit night. It was Dom Jean de Puniet who wrote in his book on the origin of the Mass that when Christ instituted the mystery of the Eucharist He was holding in one hand the chain of the old covenant which ended in Him, and in the other the first link of an unbroken chain reaching unto eternity.

§ 3

The Holy Week of the Eastern Church is marked by a number of ceremonies whose roots go back no man can say how far into the history of Christianity. They crowd one upon the other and are held all over Jerusalem in the churches of the various communities, so that it would be difficult to attend them all.

On the Saturday before Palm Sunday, Lazarus Saturday, the Greeks and the Armenians go in solemn procession to the Holy Sepulcher and the Russians hold an all-night service in their cathedral, where palms are blessed and distributed.

On Palm Sunday the most remarkable ceremonies to a Western Christian are those of the Armenians and the Syrians. The Armenians perform "the Ceremony of the Second Coming." Every picture and decoration in the church of St. James is covered with a veil, and the altar is concealed behind a tapestry. A bishop stands holding a key which symbolizes the key of the church, while another bishop, invisible to the congregation, stands behind the tapestry, and there begins a dialogue between them, one asking for admittance and the other asking who it is that calls. Finally the Bishop outside chants: "Open unto me the gates of righteousness that I may enter into them and give thanks unto the Lord!" Slowly the curtain is withdrawn, and at the same moment the veils are drawn from the pictures, and the church, hitherto dark and shrouded, shines with candle-light.

The Syrian ceremony, which is almost the same and quite as protracted, is called "the Ceremony of the Bridegroom's Arrival." The altar of the church is concealed from the congregation by draperies. The Bishop and clergy go round the church in procession, halting before the curtain. Forty times the worshipers make a complete prostration lying full length on the ground. At length the Bishop cries, "O Lord, O Lord, O Lord, open unto us!" and at that moment the curtain is drawn, revealing the altar blazing with candles.

On Maundy Thursday the Greeks, Latins, Armenians, Syrians and Copts all observe the curious ceremony, rather like a miracle play, called "the Washing of the Feet." On

Good Friday the Russians perform the touching "Ceremony of the Winding-Sheet." A shroud is placed on the altar, and after the service, while a choir sings "the Hymn of the Myrrh-bearers," the priests lift the winding sheet, carry it three times around the altar and then to a sepulcher prepared in the church, where it is censed.

A curious and interesting service is the Good Friday "Entombment" of the Syrians. The Bishop, carrying a crucifix and followed by the clergy, marches around the church to commemorate the approach to Golgotha. Having reached a table that represents the place of Crucifixion, they place the crucifix on it, and put two candles, one on each side, to represent the crosses of the two thieves. The Bishop wraps a scarlet cloth round the crucifix to suggest the covering of our Lord before He was stripped of His garments. Then, as the service proceeds, the story of the Crucifixion is read from one of the Gospels. When they reach the incident of the two thieves, one of the candles, that representing the impenitent thief, is broken, and as the story of the death of Christ is read the crucifix is censed, lifted on high, and held to the four corners of the earth while a blessing is pronounced.

The crucifix is placed in a special coffin and carried to the altar. It is there washed in rose water in which is a quantity of gall, and then it is tenderly wrapped in linen with powdered incense and replaced in the coffin. This touching and simple act of symbolism is concluded when the Bishop escorts the coffin to a place behind the altar where it is locked away and a seal placed on the door. A lamp is left burning in front of it all night and on Easter Eve the tomb is opened.

Saturday, Easter Eve, is the day for the ceremony of the Holy Fire, which I will describe in its place. On the same day, but late at night, the dark monks of the Abyssinian Church celebrate one of the most primitive and most spectacular of all the ceremonies: "Searching for the Body of Christ."

§ 4

I was told to rise at five A.M. if I wanted to see anything of the Greek ceremony of the Washing of the Feet, which takes place at eight A.M. in the courtyard of the Holy Sepulcher. For all the ceremonies of Holy Week it is necessary to be in your place two or three hours before anything is timed to happen, and, as nearly everything begins late, you are often there for much longer. But the crowd is so varied and so interesting that the time passes swiftly.

I found myself perched above the wall of the Greek Chapel of St. Mary Magdalene, from which I looked straight down into the courtyard. Although it was not yet six o'clock, the courtyard and the adjoining roofs were so crowded that it did not seem possible that one more person could be admitted. Yet when I looked toward the entrance to the courtyard I saw a steady pressing forward, and realized that, impossible as it seemed, a new stream of people was forcing its way into the already overcrowded space. There is a mosque at the back whose minaret overlooks the courtyard, and I was amused to notice a veiled woman on the little railed-in gallery where the muezzin calls to prayer, crouched with two or three children and enjoying the best view of all.

The Christian crowd that comes to Jerusalem for Holy

166 .

Week is a puzzling one. It is dominated by excitable Copts from Egypt, many of whom wear bright blue gowns and a scarlet tarbush. There are also any number of Christian Arabs who dress and look exactly like the Moslems. There are also Christian *fellahin*. Added to these are numbers of Greeks, Armenians, Syrians and, here and there, a dark-skinned Ethiopian. Those are the eastern pilgrims. The western pilgrims include Catholic monks, bands of pilgrims from England, Italy and sometimes Spain, and crowds of Europeans and Americans, touring either in droves or in ones and twos, who are almost impossible to classify. Anyhow, a gathering more oddly representative of the international character of Christianity could be seen nowhere else.

In the center of the courtyard a platform had been erected. It was painted green, and there was an iron rail all around it and two iron arches, one at each end, which held old-fashioned candle lamps. There was a gilded chair at one end of the platform and along each side, flanking it, were seats for twelve priests.

This platform represented the Upper Room of the Last Supper. While a Greek priest busied himself with a long-necked ewer, a bowl and a towel, placing them carefully on the platform, another priest lowered an olive branch on a rope from a near-by wall. This branch symbolized the Garden of Gethsemane.

The procession came slowly from the Church of the Holy Sepulcher toward the platform, moving through a path made by the police. Earnest Copts and devout pilgrims, in their anxiety to touch him, nearly tore to pieces the old Greek Patriarch. He walked slowly behind his clergy, grasping his pastoral staff in one hand, while in the other he

· 167

held a posy of flowers which now and again he dipped in holy water and sprinkled on the people. He wore a dome-shaped crown sparkling with precious stones. His staff was not the crozier of the western Church, but a gold staff whose head was formed of two twined serpents: the rod of Aaron. Before him walked twelve elderly Greek priests in gorgeous copes of figured brocade.

They took places on the stage, the old Patriarch going to the chair at the head and the twelve priests seating themselves in two rows. The intention was clear. The Patriarch represented Jesus, and the twelve were His apostles.

After a short service the old man was undressed slowly and laboriously before the silent, wondering crowd. His great crown of jewels was removed, the pectoral decorations were taken from him, and then his heavy vestments were removed over his head and, behold, he stood revealed in a silk gown of pale lavender. I admired the simplicity with which he did all this, because there is something that can be so ridiculous about undressing, especially the undressing of someone as decorative as a Greek Patriarch. But very simply, as if he had been at home, he arranged his white beard and patted the soft white locks that blew about in the early wind of morning. I thought to myself that this is probably the only occasion when a crowd sees the Greek Patriarch, so to speak, *en déshabille,* because even in death the Orthodox Patriarchs, clothed in gorgeous vestments, are carried to the grave tied in their chairs and lowered into a vault where about twenty-four of their number sit clothed in the moldering relics of their glory.

The old man girded himself with a towel, another was laid over his shoulder, and, with white hair blowing in the wind, he knelt slowly and heavily toward the feet of his clergy. Black lace-up boots and elastic-sided boots were shyly removed, so were white socks, and one by one the feet were washed in the water from the gold ewer and dried with the Patriarch's towel.

When he came to the priest who represented St. Peter, there was a piece of dumb show. "Thou shalt never wash my feet," says St. Peter. "If I wash thee not, thou hast no part with me," is the answer. Eventually the Apostle gives way and the Patriarch ministers to him.

When the feet-washing is over, the scene is changed to the Garden of Gethsemane. Three of the clergy, representing Peter, James and John, pretend to fall asleep on the steps of the platform. The Patriarch goes some distance off. He returns to tell them that Judas is at hand. The Patriarch is robed again in his splendid vestments and stands on the platform blessing the congregation. As the procession is re-formed, the gong of the Holy Sepulcher begins to ring a strange exciting rhythm:

Dong-dong-dong
a-dong-dong-dong
dong-a-dong-dong
dong-dong-dong.

It is a strange rhythm on one note. The deep-voiced gong seems to shake the very stones. The crowds press forward for the Patriarch's blessing. He holds the little posy of flowers in his hand, a tight little Victorian posy of small flowers, and, dipping it in holy water he shakes the drops into the faces of the crowd.

§ 5

By courtesy of the Armenian Patriarch I was given a seat in the Armenian Gallery in the Church of the Holy Sepulcher, and was told to be in my place four hours before the ceremony of the Holy Fire would begin. The approaches to the church were full of excited people, and it was with some difficulty that I struggled through the crowds who had been waiting inside the church all night.

My seat looked directly down on the Tomb and gave a good view of the Rotunda, which was a tight press of people. The eastern Christians, and many of them seemed to be Copts and Syrians, have little reverence in our sense of the word, and therefore perhaps it may be unkind to criticize them from our western standpoint. They see nothing shocking in screaming, fighting and shouting around the Tomb of Christ or in trampling each other to the ground in a frenzied dash for the fire which they believe comes straight from heaven.

Hundreds had slept all night in the church. Beneath the columns which support the central dome, wooden scaffolding had been erected which formed a series of little boxes like those in a theater. Most of them seemed to be occupied by rich Copts. They rested cross-legged on cushions, surrounded by their families. Mothers feeding their infants sat on the bedding. The men sat in front of the boxes slowly telling rosaries of yellow amber or excitedly arranging to lower a bunch of candles on a string to be lit by someone in the crowd when the great moment should arrive.

The crowd moved uneasily. Something was always happening in it; either someone was madly fighting to escape from it or else someone was fighting as madly to enter it. Christian Arabs, mounted on the shoulders of their friends, swayed above the heads of the crowd and beat time with their hands or with sticks as they chanted:

> The Fire has shone and we have feasted,
> We have visited the sepulcher of our Lord,
> Our Lord is Jesus Christ.
> Christ came to us and with His blood He bought us.

Looking at the crowd as it became more and more excited, I understood why no Jew would dare to come near the Holy Sepulcher on the day of the Holy Fire.

Time and again the crowds have been told that the Holy Fire is a piece of symbolism, but nothing will shake their belief that it descends into the Tomb of Christ from heaven. The ceremony is very old. I believe it was mentioned by Bernard the Monk who saw it when he visited Jerusalem in the year 870 A.D.

Suddenly the excitement reached its highest point as police, hitting out with sticks and cudgels, forced a way into the church for the patriarchs and the clergy of the various communities. While what looked like a riot was in progress below, I noticed that on each side of the Tomb are two circular openings set aslant in the stone. These openings are blackened by the Holy Fire of other years and at them runners stood, stripped for their ordeal and holding bunches of candles protected by caps of perforated tin. Instantly the fire appeared, these men had to light their candles and fight their way out of the church where friends were waiting in motor cars to rush the sacred flame to churches all over the country. In the old days a ship was always ready with steam up to take the Holy Fire to Russia.

Then the great moment arrived. In noisy excitement the Greek and the Armenian patriarchs were conducted to the entrance of the Tomb. In full view of the shouting, screaming crowds, the old Greek Patriarch was divested of his rich cope and other ornaments. His wrists were tied with linen bands. The old man then turned and entered the Tomb, while the Armenian Patriarch waited in the vestibule.

There were three or four minutes in which nothing happened. The air was tight with suspense. Suddenly came a burst of flame from each of the Tomb openings, one torch being thrust out by the Greek Patriarch, and the other by the Armenian. The next instant the church was a shrieking, stamping madness. Tongues of flame swept over it. Men fought to escape with the fire. The crowds lit candle from candle, laughing with joy. Some moved the flames over their faces. Women passed it under their chins and over their breasts. The people in the galleries hauled up lit candles on strings, and in the inconceivable pandemonium the ancient figure of the Greek Patriarch emerged from the Tomb, grasping a lighted candle in each hand, and was swept onward like a piece of driftwood on a flooded river.

While the crowds went mad with the fire, the bells of the church began to ring and the strange wooden gongs of the Armenians were beaten with strips of metal in the gallery. The whole church was a chaos of sound and movement. In the utter confusion of the moment all the lamps were rekindled in the Holy Sepulcher and hundreds of simple, but apparently mad, Christians believed that God had sent fire from heaven.

I sat there for an hour after the appearance of the fire, watching the excitement of the crowds. The fire did not appear to burn them as they licked the flames and ran them over their faces, neither did it singe their hair. I thought what an extraordinary thing it is that a frenzied ceremony that might have occurred in a grove of Adonis should have taken place at the Tomb of Christ.

§ 6

A friend who lives in Jerusalem offered to take me to the strangest of all the ceremonies of the Eastern Holy Week. It is held by the black monks of Abyssinia on the roof of the Holy Sepulcher.

As the moon was rising, a Greek monk let us into the church by a side door. It was pitch dark. We had to strike matches as we stumbled up over worn stairs to the roof of St. Helena's Chapel, where the black monks worship Christ under the stars. Long years ago, the Abyssinians owned important shrines within the Sepulcher, but during centuries of struggle they were unable to hold out against more powerful Churches and so, bit by bit, they found themselves dislodged and driven from their sacred heritage. But, with a tenacity which has enabled these devout men to retain their faith since the fourth century, they sought refuge on the roof.

Lacking a church large enough to hold a big ceremony, they erect a tent in which once every year they celebrate a

curious rite known as "Searching for the Body of Christ."
This was the ceremony we had come to witness.

We found ourselves in bright starlight. The white domes
gave to the roof the appropriate appearance of an African
village. A long, brocade tent like a marquee had been set
up in one corner, the flaps at one end looped up so that we
could see inside, where, in a warm glow of candlelight, sat a
barbaric assembly of Abyssinians dressed in gorgeous robes,
with spiked gold crowns upon their heads. These were the
cross bearers.

A black monk led us to a row of cane-bottomed chairs at
the end of the tent. Here we sat for a long time, watching
the grave, dignified row of Abyssinians in their splendid
vestments. They looked like the pictures of the Magi.

After perhaps half an hour we heard the discordant African chanting and into the tent came the monks, leading the
Abouna, or abbot, to his place.

On the ground in front of him sat two monks with large
silver-rimmed drums which they played with a quick hand-
slapping motion, while the others shook sistra, filling the
tent with an extraordinary shivering sound like the noise
of shaken coins. The sistrum is a metal frame with hori-
zontal rods placed through it. These rods jingle when
shaken and make a sound which was known in the temples
of Ancient Egypt. It was believed able to drive away evil
spirits.

The tapping of the drums, the shivering of the sistra and
the harsh chanting of the black monks made it difficult to
believe that one was attending a Christian ceremony. Yet
there was something impressive in the sight of these black
men worshiping Jesus with a ritual so old that it has bor-

rowed something from the ceremonies of ancient Israel and Egypt.

Suddenly a sad wailing rose up from them. My friend whispered that they were bewailing the death of Jesus. The drum taps became slower and the notes of the sistra grew faint. The Gospels were brought to the abbot who, standing beneath a state umbrella, intoned the story of the Passion while monks puffed incense around him. Then the drums grew quicker, and the monks and all of us who were watching took two lighted candles and, forming up two by two, went out in the light of the full moon to search for the Body of Christ.

This rite is really a simple dramatization of the Resurrection. The abbot had read the Gospel story up to the point where the three Marys had gone to the rock-hewn tomb early in the morning with sweet spices to anoint the dead body of the Saviour. There they saw a young man sitting clothed in a white garment, and he told them that Christ was risen. . . .

And now the black monks took up the story and acted it. With a queer sidelong, dancing shuffle they gyrated around the roof in the moonlight, crying that the tomb was empty, wailing because Jesus was dead, pretending to search for His Body in the dark shadows of the roof. Each monk held a lighted candle and the abbot walked under his green and gold umbrella.

The full moon was up, shining over Jerusalem, striking shivers of green and red light from the jeweled crowns of the cross bearers. And so the fantastic assembly moved in a weird ritual dance to the sound of tom-toms and sistra.

On the fourth time around the tom-toms ceased, but the

sistra continued to vibrate. The wailing went on and on. I remembered the words of the angels to Mary Magdalene:

"Woman, why weepest thou?

"She saith unto them, Because they have taken away my Lord, and I know not where they have laid Him."

These black men, performing their ancient rite on the roof of Christ's tomb, were expressing in their own outwardly barbaric way the sorrow of all Christianity in the death of Jesus Christ.

Suddenly the wailing stopped. In silence the black monks re-entered the tent and grouped themselves around the Abbot. We slipped away quietly.

"They will remain sad until the morning," whispered my friend. "Then they will celebrate the Resurrection and become as happy as they are now miserable."

We went down through the dark church into the sleeping streets of Jerusalem.

CHAPTER SEVEN

§ 1

When Jesus came through the excited countryside and climbed up to Jerusalem, we know that He went many times to the Mount of Olives to meditate and to mourn. He was mourning not for Jerusalem the city, but for Jerusalem the Sanctuary. He knew how debased and formalized the worship of God had become, how cynical and worldly were the priests, led by a High Priest who on great occasions officiated with silk gloves so that his hands should not be stained. They were men gorged with the riches of the world, in whose hearts observance had replaced faith.

Every evening as He went across the Mount of Olives to Bethany, where He stayed outside the city, He would upon turning have seen the great Temple in the southern angle of the wall of Jerusalem, and in the morning as He came down the mountain toward Jerusalem He would see the celebrated House of God beginning the sacrifices and observances of the day. The Temple was Jerusalem, and, to strict Jews everywhere in the world, Jerusalem meant only the Temple.

What was this Temple like in the time of Jesus? What happened there? What would we have seen above those white walls, could we have gone with the Master from the Garden of Gethsemane to the higher places of the Hill? First of all, the Temple was, to the Jew, God's house. It had grown out of the Tabernacle in which long ages before Moses had kept the Ark of the Covenant and the Tables of the Law. This tabernacle was a large and splendid tent, or marquee, which the Israelites took about with them during their wandering in the wilderness, erecting it every time they chose a new camping ground. When they invaded Palestine and settled down, ceasing to be nomads, it was decided to erect the Tabernacle in some material more durable than cloth and the skins of animals. Therefore Solomon built the Temple in stone but it remained essentially a reproduction, although of a much larger scale, of the ancient Tabernacle of Moses.

It was served by an enormous number of priests and attendants. While it was still dark the Temple guards patrolled the gates and courts in twenty-four stations. Each station consisted of ten Levites, so that two hundred and forty watchers were on duty every night. During the night the "Captain of the Temple" went his rounds and visited all the posts. The Romans divided the night into four watches, the Jews into three. Anyone standing on the Mount of Olives in the third Jewish watch would have seen the huge building wrapped in silence and darkness, the only light a red glow in the center of the white terraces where the fire on the altar of burnt offerings was kept alight day and night.

The priests who were selected to offer the daily morning sacrifice slept in a room in the inner court. In the third watch, while it was still dark, they would awaken and take a ceremonial bath to be in readiness for the casting of the lots. An official would come to them, still in the hours of darkness, and cast lots to decide the priest who would remove the ash from the altar of burnt offering. This man, alone and with no light but that of the altar flames, would go out and wash his hands and feet in the brazen laver that stood before the altar. He did this by placing the right hand on the left foot and the left hand on the right foot. He then mounted the huge altar of unhewn stone with a silver chafing dish in his hand, into which he swept the ashes; and as he descended he would see in the renewed glow of firelight the other priests ascending with shovels and prongs to place fresh wood on the flames.

Then came the second casting. The president would range the priests before him and cast lots to decide:

> who was to slaughter the victim;
> who was to sprinkle blood on the altar;
> who was to remove ashes from the altar of incense;
> who was to trim the lamps on the seven-branched candlestick;
> who was to carry the head of the sacrifice and a hind leg;
> who the two forelegs;
> who the tail and the other hind leg;
> who the breast and the neck;
> who the two sides;
> who the entrails;
> who the offering of flour;
> who the baked-meat offering of the High Priest;
> who the wine and the drink offering.

When this had been decided the time had come to watch for the first hint of sunrise. One of the priests climbed to a pinnacle of the Temple and stood gazing toward the East in the grayness of the morning. The president and the priests waited below for his report. When his cry came down to them, "The morning shineth already," they would ask him, "Is the sky lit up as far as Hebron?" and not until he had agreed would the daily sacrifice begin.

The sacrificial lamb, that had lived for four days in a special room in the Temple and had already been examined for any of the numerous blemishes that would unfit it for death, was led out and again examined by the light of torches. It was given a drink from a golden bowl. Ninety-three sacred utensils were brought from a room near by and the lamb was led to the altar. The forefeet and hindfeet of each side were tied together and the head was placed through a ring in the ground, the face turned to the west.

At this moment, as the first light of a new day began to pulse upward from behind the Mount of Olives, the signal was given to open the Temple gate. As the gate moved the priests lifted silver trumpets and uttered the three shrill calls that announced every morning to Jerusalem that the sacrifice was ready to be slain.

At the same moment, the two priests who had been chosen to attend to the altar of incense and the lamps ascended the steps of the Holy Place and entered to perform their duty. The opening of this gate was the signal for the sacrifice. One priest drew the lamb's gullet forward while he thrust in the knife with an upward movement. Another priest caught the blood in a golden bowl and, standing at the east of the altar, sprinkled the blood on the stones. The victim was then unbound and flayed. The entrails were washed on marble tables and the carcass was cut into pre-scribed portions, each one carried by the priest to whose lot it had fallen. These portions were borne to the rise of the altar, where they were salted. The most solemn part of the sacrifice was then ready to begin.

The priests gathered once more in the Hall of Polished Stones to cast lots for the one who should officiate at the altar of incense in the Holy Place. He had to be a priest who had never before performed this office, unless, of course, everyone present had done so. He then chose two assistants, and while on his way to the Holy Place struck a great gong called the Magrephah at whose sound the vast Temple became alive with priests and Levites and ordinary worshipers gathering to pray. Meanwhile the three incense priests entered the Holy Place. One spread the coals on the golden altar. The other made ready the incense. They then withdrew, leaving the officiating priest waiting for the signal to burn the incense.

At this moment silence fell over the vast Temple. The worshipers "fell down before the Lord." Clouds of dense, sweet smoke rose from the Holy Place. Solemnly the priests gathered around the altar to place the portions of the burnt offering in the flames. Then followed the two meat offerings and the drink offerings, and as the priest was bending forward to pour out the drink the Levites broke into the psalm of the day. At each pause in the music the priests blew twice on their silver trumpets and the worshipers prostrated themselves. As the flames licked the newly slain meat, burning brightly with the oil and the salt, the morning sacrifice in the Temple was over.

§2

Day by day for centuries the same thing went on. Thousands of beasts and birds atoned for the sins of humanity at the altar of the Lord. Blood flowed in a never-ending stream, and the smell of the Temple was the stench of burning fat. In addition to the routine sacrifices, thousands of private individuals offered sheep, goats, and oxen. They brought forward their victims, placed their whole weight on them to symbolize the substitutive nature of the rite, and then slit their throats while the priests caught the blood. But that was all the Temple had to offer. It gave no spiritual direction. It was merely a sacred shambles. Isaiah sounded its death-knell centuries before the time of Christ: "For what purpose is the multitude of your sacrifices to me, saith the Lord," he cried. "I am full of burnt offerings of rams and the fat of fed beasts; and I delight not in the blood of bullocks, or of lambs or of he-goats." From that time the spiritual history of the Jew was locked up not in the Temple but in the synagogue. The Roman who thought that in destroying the Temple he was destroying Judaism was wrong, because Judaism was no longer there.

Much has been written about the attitude of Jesus to the Temple. We cannot doubt that while He reverenced the thing it stood for, He condemned the thing it had become. "I will have mercy and not sacrifice," He said. His opinion of the priesthood was well expressed in the Parable of the Good Samaritan, and one might perhaps read into His attack on the money changers and the merchants in the Temple a deeper meaning than a dislike for the carrying on of business in a sacred place. Was it not also a protest against the whole financial system of the Temple?

But what was this system? The priests literally raked in the shekels and lived, quite as literally, on the fat of the land. The Temple Tribute, or poll tax, was only one of the imposts levied on the Jews for the upkeep of the Temple. Offerings of a different nature embraced every conceivable thing.

There were the first fruits, the so-called "seven kinds," which were wheat, barley, vines, figs, pomegranates, olives and honey. Those near Jerusalem offered them fresh to the Temple; those far away brought them dried. Philo and the Mishna describe how the villagers assembled together at the time of the offering of the first fruits and came up to Jerusalem to the music of the pipes, the procession led by a sacrificial ox with gilded horns garlanded with olive leaves.

In addition to the first fruits were the *terumah,* an offering of wheat, wine, and oil; the *challah,* an offering of kneaded dough; and the oppressive tithes which, says the Mishna, covered "everything which may be used as food and is cultivated, growing out of the earth." It was this rigorous system of taxing the most humble crops, such as mint and anise and cummin, that provoked Jesus to cry out: "but woe unto you, Pharisees, for ye tithe mint and rue and all manner of herbs, and pass over judgement and the love of God."

Then there was the offering of all first-born sons and all the male first-born of animals. The sons were ransomed on payment of five shekels to the Temple Treasury, and a lesser money payment was made for the first-born males among the non sacrificial animals, such as the ass, the horse, and the camel. But the first-born of goats and sheep and oxen belonged to the Temple.

In addition to all this the priests received incredible quantities of meat. All kinds of sacrifices followed each other at the altar: sin offerings, trespass offerings, meat offerings, thank offerings, and burnt offerings. From all except the last, which were entirely consumed on the altar, the priests received a good share of the meat for their private use. In sin offerings, for instance, only the fat was thrown on the altar, and the priests received a proportion of the carcass. In thank offerings they were entitled to the breast and right shoulder—and even in burnt offerings the skins fell to them, in which they did a profitable business.

Therefore the Temple must have been an enormous storehouse of every kind of food and produce. Its vaults were stacked with the very best that the country could grow. In them also were large gold deposits, for, like most temples in ancient times, it was a bank in the sense that it offered strong rooms and safe deposits for the wealthy.

It was this mighty institution which Christ entered with a whip in His hand. The market was a remarkable feature of the Temple. During the days before the Passover, it was at its busiest. It was a cattle market. It was a money market. It was also possible to buy the necessary food and drink offerings there. The market had no doubt grown up over a long period of time because of the demand for Levitically perfect animals, the need to change money into Sanctuary coin, and a hundred other material matters connected with the Temple worship. What a thriving trade was done there may be imagined when we realize that even animals offered for sacrifice had first to be passed by an inspector. If it was

184 ·

of the wrong age or sex or was wrongly marked or otherwise flawed, it was rejected. There was no trouble, however, if the purchaser went to the cattle market inside the
Temple area where the animals had already been passed and
were sold at higher prices, of course, with a guarantee that
they were acceptable to God.

The market was held under the arcades in the great Court
of the Gentiles. It must have been like any market in Damascus or Jerusalem or Cairo today: a tense mass of arguing,
bargaining people. Many a poor peasant was well fleeced
there. We know that prices were artificially maneuvered
and that on one occasion the cost of two pigeons was run up
to the ridiculous price of a gold denar, or about $2.50 of
modern money but before night it had fallen, through the
intervention of an honest man, to the normal charge of a
quarter of a silver denar, or about thirty cents.

When Jesus entered the Temple Market it must have
been loud with the bleating of the sacrificial lambs in their
pens, the lowing of cattle and the cooing of doves. Men
must have been arguing loudly, laughing, trying to get the
better of each other, and gazing with contempt on the poor
pilgrim who offered no man a profit.

There is an interesting point about this market. There
is reason to think that it was the property of Annas, who
had been High Priest for many years. This was the place
known as "the bazaars of the sons of Annas," and Josephus
makes the significant remark that Annas, the son of the
Annas of the New Testament, was "a great hoarder-up of
money." If this was so, can we not see how Christ's attack
was aimed not only at the prestige of the priests but also at
their pockets and the whole financial system by which they

had grown rich? One critic has even suggested that this was one of the main reasons for the arrest of Jesus.

It is, at any rate, certain that in cleansing the Temple Jesus delivered a blow at the vested interests of the aristocratic priesthood. His action was an invitation to all honest men; and the poor, patient multitudes, who were mercilessly squeezed to support one of the most numerous and best-nourished priesthoods in history, gave Him such support in His protest that even the Temple police, who usually corrected the slightest irregularity, did not dare to lay a finger on Him. "And he taught daily in the temple," says St. Luke. "But the chief priests and the scribes and the chief of the people sought to destroy him. And could not find what they might do: for all the people were very attentive to hear him."

So the Jewish authorities who had, before the Passover, already decided to arrest Him, put their heads together and instigated the plot that led to the Cross.

§ 3

Many of those during the British rule in Palestine who witnessed the frequent Arab-Jew riots which took place during Holy Week compared the situation with that in Roman times. The Passover was always the moment when the Romans took precautions to prevent or crush any religious or nationalist revolt, and to them the disturbance which led to the Crucifixion must have seemed of that order.

Pontius Pilate did not normally live in Jerusalem. The headquarters of his government were at Caesarea on the coast. But it was his custom to move up to Jerusalem with extra troops during Passover time to be ready in the event of trouble. In precisely the same way the British Government was in the habit of drafting troops from Haifa and other places into Jerusalem at Easter time, keeping them handy and under cover in case the police needed help. Pilate had to go up to Jerusalem for still another reason. When the Romans took over the government of Judaea they confiscated the ceremonial vestments of the high priest and locked them up in a stone room in the castle of Antonia next to the Temple. The idea was of course to drive home to those powerful and arrogant functionaries that they held their sacerdotal privileges by the will of Rome. So every year at Passover time the Roman governor had to go to Jerusalem and officially hand over to the high priest his sacred vestments whose fringes were sewn with little bells.

The Passover was a happy but tumultuous feast. The excitability and instability of the crowds which thronged Jerusalem at that time are clearly reflected in the Gospels. At one moment they cried "Hosanna"; at the next, "Crucify him!"

I had hardly expected to be so vividly reminded of this by a modern crowd, yet every time I went out into the streets and saw Jews, Christians and Moslems each excited by their own religious festivals I thought to myself "This is the same atmosphere described by Matthew, Mark, Luke and John." The rich Jews from England and the United States, who had come to attend the Passover and to see how Zionism was progressing, might have been the counterparts of the wealthy Jews of Alexandria and Antioch who voyaged to the Holy City in the time of Jesus. Whenever I met processions in the streets, solemn groups of men and women holding candles and intoning a psalm, or when I came across hilarious processions, with drums beating and banners waving, my mind was taken far back down the centuries. Once I had to take refuge in a house from an enormous Arab gathering which advanced slowly and threateningly the whole width of the road led by a man dancing and twirling as David danced before the Ark of the Covenant, while behind him in the crowd men, mounted on the shoulders of other men, sang songs and fought each other with wooden swords.

In the time of Jesus the Passover drew enormous crowds to Jerusalem. Jews came not only from every part of Palestine, but from the great Jewish quarter of Alexandria, and even from Europe, to slay the Paschal lamb in the only place where the sacrifice could be offered: on the altar of the Temple of Herod. Gentiles from all lands also flocked to Jerusalem out of curiosity, because it was the great time to visit the city. Gabriel Miro, in his brilliant piece of fiction *Figures of the Passion of our Lord,* represents Pilate as the host of a globe-trotting houseparty of rich Romans who had come to observe the strange habits of the Jews. The book is extraordinarily lifelike and probable.

In order to convince Nero of the importance of the Jewish nation, Cestius Gallus, Governor of Syria, once counted the sacrificial lambs during the Passover and the number was 256,500. Allowing for the minimum number of ten persons for each lamb eaten at the feast, this gives us the enormous total of 2,565,000. The city was naturally full, and the pilgrims were also camped around the walls in tents.

Jesus, as we know, stayed at Bethany with His friends, and it is interesting to learn from the Talmud that among the places which were specially noted for their hospitality to pilgrims were that village and its neighbor, Bethphage.

The Passover lambs were slain on the afternoon of Nisan [April] 14, the day of the first spring full moon. In order that the thousands of animals might be slain, skinned, cleaned and cooked for the table that same evening, the afternoon Temple sacrifice was put forward an hour and the priests were free to deal with the wholesale sacrifice of lambs at 1:30 P.M. our time.

Thousands of men, each carrying a lamb across his shoulders, congested all the roads leading to the Temple. The lamb had to be without blemish, not under eight days old and not over twelve months. Each lamb had to be eaten by a company of no fewer than ten persons and not more than twenty.

The festal crowds were divided into three divisions, and each division was admitted in turn into the Temple. After the admission of a division the great gates were closed while the huge crowd and its animals were marshaled across the enormous Court of the Gentiles to the Court of the Priests. Two rows of barefoot priests in white robes lined the path to the altar of burnt offering, one row holding golden, and the other silver, bowls. Each member of the crowd slew his own lamb, and as he did so the nearest priest caught the blood in a bowl and passed it up the line, receiving an empty bowl in return. The priests at the head of the lines spilled the blood in jets at the base of the altar and the red stream ran away by underground channels into the brook Kedron. Trumpet notes rang out over the Temple to mark each sacrifice, and the Levites led the crowds in hymns of praise.

No sooner were the lambs slain than they were hung up on hooks along the Court, or suspended on staves between the shoulders of two men, and flayed. The inside fat was separated and offered with incense on the altar. The fleeces were left behind as the perquisite of the priests. Then the ceremony was repeated with the next division, and so on until hundreds of thousands of lambs had been slain.

After the great slaughter was over the priests washed the blood from the Court, while the crowds went to their homes, their lodgings, and their tents to make ready for the feast. A spit of pomegranate wood was passed through the lamb. Not one bone had to be broken, and the animal had to be roasted in an earthenware oven and carefully watched in order to prevent any part of it touching the oven. If this happened, the part touched had to be cut away and destroyed.

We can imagine how the tremendous activity, the bustle, and the excitement of the afternoon was succeeded by a Sabbath stillness as the sun fell and the pilgrims were busy with the preparation for their feast. The streets would be empty. Each householder would be at home arranging the final details. The smell of roasting meat would rise up over Jerusalem and spread even to the hills around. The last light of the sun would rest for a moment on the white marble of the Temple, touch the golden spikes on the Holy of Holies and vanish; and with darkness the oven fires on the Mount of Olives, where the Passover tents were pitched, would glow like rubies, a prophecy of the camp fires of Titus. Then, loud, imperious, and detached, the Roman

trumpets from Antonia would ring across the silence to de-
note the changing of the guard. . . .

"And in the evening He cometh with the Twelve. . . ."

§4

We can imagine, as darkness fell and before the full
moon had lifted itself above the city, how Jesus and the
Twelve came down from the Mount of Olives and entered
Jerusalem by the Water Gate. They ascended the steep
streets to the house of the Upper Room, and were shown
up to the flat white roof where an awning, or a temporary
roof, rose above them.

The greatest artists in the world have painted their conception of this scene. I suppose Leonardo da Vinci's fresco
in Milan is the most famous. But no artist has been able to
escape from his own time and show the Last Supper as it
must have been in the Upper Chamber of Ophel by the
light of the Paschal moon. The scene was a simple Eastern
meal. There would have been a low table with cushions
round it in a U-shape, in order that the table could at a
point in the meal be removed without disturbing the guests,
and replaced at another point in the meal. In the old days
it had been customary to eat the Passover, staff in hand and
dressed for a journey, symbolic of the flight from Egypt. In
the time of Jesus the Jews attended the feast in festal garments and ate lounging on a divan in a free position, leaning on the left side, in order to symbolize freedom after
bondage.

That Jesus and the Twelve reclined on cushions in this
way is proved by the fact that John, who sat next to our

Lord, was "leaning on Jesus' bosom." This would have been an ill-mannered and clumsy attitude if table and chairs had been used, but, if you have ever eaten an eastern meal, you will know that it is quite usual to lean back toward your neighbor to put a question.

The hush of a moonlit night wrapped itself about the House of the Last Supper. As the full moon rose, the light would have slanted in under the awning in green angles on the white stone. There would have been a lamp burning, a bright spark floating in olive oil, and beyond the stillness of the Upper Room the pinnacles and towers of Jerusalem would be seen lying against the stars like the city of a dream. And Jesus said: "Take eat: this is my body . . . this is my blood of the new testament which is shed for many."

"And when they had sung an hymn they went out into the Mount of Olives."

Is there in all literature a greater feeling of stillness than in this chapter of the Gospels? The last week in the life of Jesus is, so it seems to me, an extraordinary contrast of noise and peace. At one moment the shouting of a crowd comes to us over nineteen centuries, loud, violent and terrible; and at the next a hush has fallen and Christ is walking with the Twelve over the Mount of Olives. There is something awesome in the description of Jesus before the Crucifixion. The evangelists did not strive after any effect. They were interested only in setting down the most important happenings in their lives in a few simple words, yet through the stark economy of their writing shines something beyond the power of words to describe. We get the impression, Dr. Sanday has said, "that there is always a vaster consciousness

Modern Jerusalem, showing the enormous Moslem Mosque, the Dome of the Rock, which occupies the site of Solomon's temple.

Girl carrying water from the Virgin's Well under the city wall in Jerusalem.

waiting to break through." Nowhere in the Gospels is this "vaster consciousness" so evident as it is when Jesus Christ moves through hate and treachery and all the baser things and, founding His Church in gentleness and in love, walks in a ghostly calm through moonlight to the Garden of Gethsemane.

"Sit ye here while I go and pray," said Jesus and, taking Peter, James and John, He went a little way off in the shadow out of the brightness of the moon.

"My soul is exceeding sorrowful," He said, "even unto death; tarry ye here and watch with me."

And He went still deeper into the shadow.

When He came back the three Apostles had fallen asleep:

"Peter," He said. "What, could ye not watch with me one hour? Watch and pray, that ye enter not into temptation: the spirit indeed is willing, but the flesh is weak."

He went into the shadow for a second time and prayed:

"If this cup may not pass away from me, except I drink it, thy will be done."

And when He came back the second time the three were again asleep. Jesus went for a third time into the shadow, but when He came back this last time He looked down on the sleeping men and said:

"Sleep on now and take your rest."

For His hour had come, and He stood waiting in the light.

The eight disciples who had been left near the entrance to the garden had seen lamps mounted on staves swinging against the darkness of the Temple mount. These lanterns descended into the valley of the Kedron and then advanced up the slight hill toward the garden. They recognized the tramp of the Roman soldiers, who wore sandals studded with nails. They heard the excited whispering of the Jews. Although the moon was full, the approaching men came swinging their lights so that they could see into all the caves and dark places.

Judas, after he had slipped away from the Upper Room, had gone to the priests and called for a guard. The priests must have approached Pilate, for St. John says that at the head of the troops came the *chiliarch* of the Twelfth Legion, the officer commanding the Jerusalem cohort. The soldiers must have gone first to the house of the Last Supper and, finding that Jesus had left, had descended the steep streets of Ophel and crossed the Kedron, taking the same road that Jesus had taken a few hours before.

How else can one explain that strange and vivid incident in the *Gospel of St. Mark,* the incident of the young man who fled naked? Surely this could be no other than St. Mark himself, a young boy at the time. We can imagine how interested he would have been in the great Rabbi who had come to the Upper Room in his mother's house; how, when he was fast asleep that night, the tramp of the soldiers and the knocking on the door would have awakened him, filling him with curiosity and fear. Slipping a linen cloth about him, he would have crept from the house and followed the bobbing lanterns down the hill. Perhaps his eager young mind was bent on giving an alarm, on telling Jesus that men with swords and staves had been asking for Him; or possibly he was merely filled with the normal curiosity of a boy. His young figure in its linen cloth shadowed Judas and the band, sometimes stepping out of the moonlight as they paused, sometimes running on, clinging to the shadows. Unknown to anyone, he would have been watching outside the garden when Judas stepped forward and betrayed Christ. He would have seen and heard everything. He heard Judas say:

"Hail, Master."

He heard Jesus reply:

"Judas, betrayest thou the son of man with a kiss?"

He heard the sudden tumult and saw the flash of steel in the moonlight as Peter struck at Malchus, the servant of the High Priest. He heard Jesus ask:

"Whom seek ye?"

"Jesus of Nazareth," they said.

"I am he."

And when the disciples, except Peter and John, had fled, the young man, leaving his hiding place, would have followed Jesus and His captors as they went from the garden toward the dark ravine of the Kedron. It was then that the young eavesdropper was noticed by one of the soldiers, and St. Mark says:

"And a certain young man followed with him, having a linen cloth cast about him, over his naked body; and they lay hold on him; but he left the linen cloth and fled naked."

Who would have noticed this triviality during the arrest of Jesus except the man to whom it had happened?

§ 5

It was perhaps three o'clock in the morning when the guards with their Prisoner arrived at the palace of the High Priest, which stood on the slopes of the southern hill not far from the house of the Last Supper.

In the audience chamber of the palace Jesus was brought before Caiaphas and a few members of the Sanhedrin who had been drawn from their beds to attend the private inquiry.

St. John tells us that the ex-high priest, Annas, was also there. Some scholars believe that this rich and influential Jew whose family fortunes owed much to the Temple market which Jesus had condemned, may have been the chief mover in the plot. There were false witnesses, spies who had been following the Master in the Temple, whispering with Judas, listening at keyholes. But even these wretches could not agree in infamy. Jesus stood in silence watching His foes.

"Answerest Thou nothing?" cried Caiaphas.

And Jesus held His peace.

Then Caiaphas saw the way to trap Him, and administered the solemn oath:

"I adjure Thee by the living God, that Thou tell us whether Thou be the Christ, the Son of God!"

It was a command that no Jew could disobey:

"Thou hast said," replied Jesus.

Then the High Priest, rising as ordained by the Law whenever blasphemy was uttered, took his priestly garments at the neck and rent inner and outer garment so that they could never be mended. The silence of death was over the room.

"Behold, now ye have heard his blasphemy: What think ye?"

From the circle of faces came the answer:

"He is guilty of death."

Downstairs in the courtyard Peter was warming his hands at the brazier. It was now almost day. It was that gray time, the color of a dove's wing, when there are no shadows. It was the time the stars die one by one. As Peter bent over the fire, the maidservant who had let him in and the others who were warming their hands nudged each other and whispered:

"Thou also wast with Jesus of Galilee!"

And Peter drew back and said quickly:

"I know not what thou sayest!"

Uneasily, angrily, he left the fire and moved away to the porch, but there another maid saw him:

"This fellow was also with Jesus of Nazareth," she said.

"I do not know the man," cried Peter.

"Surely thou also art one of them," persisted those round the fire as they heard his Galilean accent, "for thy speech betrayeth thee?"

"I know not the man!" he cried angrily a third time.

And immediately the cock crew. It was the only sound in the stillness of the dawn. It came from the gardens on the Mount of Olives. The sharp sound was like a knife in Peter's heart. As he turned in the agony of his self-abasement, his eyes were drawn upward to the gallery where a figure in the white festal garments of the Last Supper was standing, His wrists bound with cord. Jesus turned and

looked down at Peter. And Peter went out in the cold wind
that blows before the morning, and saw the color stealing
back into the world and the sky behind the Mount of Olives
pulsing with the promise of a new day. And Peter wept.

§ 6

After their interrogation of Jesus the Chief Priest and the
rulers decided that He must die, but they had no authority
to condemn him. Although the Romans allowed the Jews
home rule under their parliament, the Sanhedrin, this body
was not allowed to inflict capital punishment without the
consent of the Roman governor. That was why early the
next morning Jesus was taken before Pilate.

St. Matthew is the only evangelist who tells us that as
Pilate was taking his seat in the law court a messenger hurried up and gave him a message from his wife. The note
begged him to have nothing to do with the condemnation
of Jesus—"that righteous man"—and that she had "suffered
many things this day in a dream because of him."

We know little else of this woman except that at the
eleventh hour she tried to save the life of Jesus. Her name
is said to have been Claudia Procula and it is believed that
she was a Roman lady of birth and influence who was related to the Emperor Tiberius. Her conduct on the morning of the Crucifixion raises a number of interesting
thoughts. Pilate must have left his palace at an unusually
early hour, at any rate before Claudia was awake, and she
was upset when, finding him already gone, she was unable
to warn him and tell him of her dreams. The only thing

she could do was to scribble the note full of haste and anxiety which she sent after him.

We can safely infer from her state of mind what is related nowhere in the Gospels: that the arrest of Jesus the night before was known to Pilate, that the danger in which He stood from the fury of the Jews was also known, and it therefore follows that someone influential enough to approach Pilate, probably the Chief Priest himself, had explained the situation and had persuaded the Governor to preside over a court in the morning—probably a day on which the courts were usually shut for it was the day before the feast—and ratify the death sentence.

If this is true, the arrest of Jesus caused a stir late at night in Pilate's household. Perhaps the Governor was called from bed to receive a report. Whatever happened it is obvious that Pilate told his wife about it, and perhaps at the same moment when St. Peter and those in the courtyard of the High Priest's house were gathered round the fire, Pilate and Claudia in their palace sat talking together of Jesus. When she retired to rest she was troubled by dreams of Him.

Pilate has suffered much from history because he was the reluctant instrument of the Crucifixion, He has been called coarse, brutal and weak-minded. But there is nothing in his record to justify these charges. It is true that he disliked the Jews for their fanaticism, their arrogance and their habit of going behind a governor's back to the central authority in Rome. This surprising glimpse of him in consultation with his wife, accessible to her advice even while he was presiding over the highest court in the land, helps to soften and humanize a character which history has cruelly condemned.

When the Jews arrived at the praetorium with their Prisoner, St. John tells us that Jesus was led inside but his accusers remained outside. This was unusual and anyone reading this account of the trial must be struck by the extraordinary fact that the judge, Pilate, was moving to and fro all the time, entering the court when he wished to speak to Jesus and going to the vestibule to speak to the Jews outside. This was probably because the Passover was ready to begin and the Jews feared that within the Gentile basilica there might lurk some fragment of leaven which they had already banished from their own homes for fear of ceremonial defilement. This leaven, or yeast, used for breadmaking at ordinary times, was considered a form of corruption and anyone in contact with it would have been debarred from taking part in the feast. "They themselves," explains St. John, "entered not into the palace, that they might not be defiled."

Pilate's willingness to comply with the Jewish taboo, inconvenient and even undignified as it was, may mean that the trial of Jesus was not a normal sitting of the Roman court but an exceptional hearing called at the request of the Jews on the Passover Eve with the object of carrying out the death sentence before the festival began. And time was running short. Only a few hours remained.

All four Gospels agree that Pilate knew that Jesus was innocent. St. Luke and St. John plainly state that thrice Pilate pronounced Him to be innocent and thrice tried to save Him from the fury and malice of His foes. Hearing that Jesus was from Galilee, Pilate sent him to Herod An-

200 .

tipas, the ruler of Galilee, who was in Jerusalem at the time. Perhaps he thought that Herod would stand up for a Galilean against the fanatical Judeans, but, if so, he was wrong. Herod was anxious to see Jesus. He had heard a lot about Him in Galilee. He was anxious for Jesus to perform a miracle before him. But as Jesus stood silent before him, Herod lost interest and, too crafty to involve himself either with Pilate or the priesthood, he returned Jesus to the Roman governor dressed in the castoff garments of a prince.

Pilate, perplexed and worried, made a second attempt to save Jesus. He offered to have him scourged and to let him go. But the mob refused the offer with shouts of rage. In the silence of the hall he asked:

"Art Thou the King of the Jews?"

The formality of the trial, the attitude of judge to prisoner, had broken down. The awe and the curiosity created by this silent Man stirred uneasily in Pilate's mind.

"My kingdom is not of this world," said Christ to Pilate.

"Art Thou a king, then?" asked Pilate.

"To this end was I born, and for this cause came I into the world, that I should bear witness unto the truth. Everyone that is of the truth heareth My voice."

Pilate looked into the eyes of Christ and expressed in three words the hunger of the pagan world:

"What is truth?"

Then Pilate, turning, went again toward the crowd in the sunlight beyond the portico. He stood there, a white figure, on the steps. When the shouting had died down, he said:

"I find in Him no fault at all."

The hatred of the crowd beat up against him like fire.

He looked into faces twisted with rage. Then a third attempt to appease them came into his mind. It was his duty to release a Passover prisoner. He offered them the choice between Jesus of Nazareth and Barabbas, a zealot who had committed murder, never doubting that they would prefer Jesus.

"But the chief priests moved the people that he should rather release Barabbas unto them."

"What will ye then that I shall do unto Him whom ye call the King of the Jews?" asked Pilate.

It was an ironic request. Up to that moment he had no intention of taking the advice of the ugly crowd.

"Crucify Him!" they shouted.

Pilate turned away and gave orders for the scourging—"the intermediate death." The punishment was either delivered by lictors with thin elm rods, or by soldiers with the horrible *flagellum,* a short whip whose leather thongs were weighted with rough fragments of metal. Pilate had no lictors.

In a short while the waiting crowds saw two figures on the steps beneath the portico. Christ stood there, a crown of thorns on His head and over His bleeding shoulders a red military cloak. Beside Him stood Pilate:

"*Ecce homo* . . . behold the Man," said Pilate.

There was no contempt in his voice. They were the words of a fair-minded man who hoped that the piteous spectacle of the scourged Christ would soften the savage hearts of His enemies. "*Ecce Homo!*" The sight is one that has roused the pity and the love of the Christian world; but to the Jews who fought and screamed that morning in Jerusalem it meant nothing. The cries "Crucify Him!" rose louder than ever. The suffering Christ was led away into the darkness of the praetorium and Pilate faced the crowd alone:

"Take *ye* Him and crucify Him!" he cried, "for I find no fault in Him!"

Once again he wasted his irony on them. He knew how they were trying to burden him with the penalty of their hate, and he told them to do the impossible. Only he could crucify, and in those words he refused. Once again the awe which the silent, suffering Christ had awakened in his heart returned and, leaving the Jews shouting for the blood of Christ, he went again into the praetorium, and once again judge and Prisoner spoke together, and it was the judge who was frightened. Pilate looked into the suffering eyes beneath the crown of thorns:

"Whence art Thou?" he asked.

He seemed to be thinking: "I know that this is no ordinary man. There is something about Him that I do not understand. He is outside my experience of men. It is my duty to save Him from the howling savages outside. Who is He? What is His mystery?"

"Whence art Thou?" he asked.

The only answer was a glance from the eyes of the Lonely Man:

"Speakest Thou not unto me?" pleaded Pilate. "Knowest Thou not that I have power to crucify Thee, and—have power to release Thee?"

In the silence of the judgment hall, with the guard standing round, Jesus spoke to Pilate at last:

"Thou couldst have no power at all against Me, except

it were given thee from above: therefore he that delivered Me unto thee hath the greater sin."

Pilate looked at Christ. He turned again to the portico and stood on the steps facing the Jews. "Pilate sought to release Him," says St. John. Then a new sound came from the crowd. No longer did they shriek "Crucify Him!" They threatened Pilate.

"If thou let this Man go, thou art not Caesar's friend!

"Whosoever maketh himself a king speaketh against Caesar!"

Then for the first time Pilate knew that the Jews had beaten him. He was not a great enough man to stand up against blackmail. It was no trivial taunt. Pilate did not underestimate the underground influence of the Jews, and there was probably much in his record that he wished to hide. His resistance collapsed, broken down by self-interest and fear.

He ascended the judgment seat, which was set on the pavement.

"Behold your King!" he said.

Jesus stood before them with blood on His brow and the stripes of the *flagellum* staining His body.

"Shall I crucify your King?" asked Pilate.

It was his last futile plea. The sight of Jesus must have wrung it from him.

"We have no king but Caesar!" came the hypocritical cry from Annas and Caiaphas and the chief men. They had twisted a charge of blasphemy into one of politics and, having failed to win their point, they had probed around to the self-interest of the judge and had turned events so that the judge now stood in the dock with the Prisoner. The ac-

cusers were too cunning for him and he gave way. He
called for a bowl of water and, before them all, he washed
his hands so that his action could be seen, even if his words
were not heard in the tumult of the crowd:

"I am innocent of the blood of this just Person: see ye
to it."

Then answered all the people and said, "His blood be
on us and on our children."

Pilate solemnly pronounced the horrible words:

"*Ibis ad crucem.*"

Then the soldiers of the Governor took Jesus into the
common hall.

§ 7

Four forms of capital punishment were recognized by the
Jews: stoning, burning, beheading, and strangling. Stoning
was the most usual. The victim was flung from a high place
and, if still alive, was stoned until dead. The Jews never
crucified living persons. There is evidence, however, that
they crucified the corpses of blasphemers and idolaters. The
men were exhibited with their faces to the people, women
with their faces to the cross, or "tree."

Death by crucifixion was originally an eastern punishment. It was practiced by the Persians, the Egyptians, and
the Phoenicians. With them also it was the custom to crucify dead bodies as a mark of contempt, as Polycrates was
crucified after suffering a death too terrible for Herodotus
to describe.

It is believed that the Romans adopted crucifixion from
the Carthaginians, who were among the most cruel of all
the ancient peoples. It was a death from which Roman

citizens were exempt, although rare instances are recorded in Sicily and Spain in which Romans were condemned to the cross. Cicero said that no word was too terrible to describe a man who had condemned a Roman citizen to such an end. Crucifixion was, therefore, a punishment reserved for slaves and for provincial malefactors.

There were three kinds of crosses: the *crux decussata* shaped like an X, also called the *crux Andreana,* because it was on this form of cross that St. Andrew was crucified at Patræ; the *crux commissa,* or St. Anthony's Cross, which was shaped like the letter T; and the *crux immissa* of Christian tradition, which had a head-piece projecting above the crossbar.

Halfway up the upright wood of the cross was a slight projection known as the *sedile,* or seat, or as the *cornu,* or horn. This took part of the victim's weight, which would otherwise have been too great to have depended entirely on the outstretched hands. It is not known whether there was a footrest. Sometimes, it appears, the victim's feet were nailed to the cross, at others it seems they were merely bound with cords. Death was always a lingering doom. The victim was left to sob the days away, exposed to the sun, torn by pain, hunger, and thirst, until his executioners, becoming weary of his agony, dispatched him with the *crurifragium,* or the breaking of the legs.

Crucifixions were always executed outside city gates and in prominent places near high roads in order that publicity might be given to the agony of the condemned and to the crime for which he had been sentenced. It was quite usual to leave the main upright of the cross in position on a recognized place of execution and the only other portion necessary, the cross beam, was carried by the victim on his shoulders to the place of death. Artists are wrong in picturing Jesus bowed beneath the weight of the entire cross. No man could have attempted to carry a cross, and after the terrible ordeals through which He had passed even the cross beam was too heavy for His strength.

Most modern artists err also in giving too great a height to the cross. It was considered sufficient if the victim's feet just cleared the ground. If the cross on which Jesus suffered had been as high as most artists imagine, it would not have been possible for the soldier to have offered the sponge of vinegar on a short reed.

In Jerusalem a society of charitable women provided a merciful drug for those about to be crucified. It was given just before the victim, stretched on the ground, was nailed to the cross beam. The inspiration for this act of compassion was the ordinance in *Proverbs,* chapter thirty-one, verse six:

"Give strong drink unto him that is ready to perish."

It is believed that the potion offered by these women was a mixture of wine and drugs, including frankincense, laudanum, myrrh, resin, saffron and mastich. This is "the wine mingled with myrrh," mentioned by St. Mark. It was offered to Jesus before the Crucifixion, but "He received it not."

In Judea the usual practice of crucifixion was modified in deference to the Jewish law, which forbade a victim to hang on the cross all night. The bodies had, therefore, to be taken down before evening in order that the ground might not suffer pollution, because everyone who suffered death on "the tree" was, according to *Deuteronomy,* accursed.

This explains the haste in which Jesus was condemned and executed, the early trial before Pilate, and the breaking of the thieves' legs in the early afternoon. Additional urgency was felt on this occasion because at six P.M. on the evening of the Crucifixion the Sabbath of Paschal week began.

The most shameful symbol of the ancient world has become the sacred emblem of the Christian Faith. In the days of the early Church the first Christians defended the cross from the sneers of the pagan by pointing out its universal presence in Nature and in everyday life: the wings of a flying bird, the branches of trees, the projecting oars of galleys, the ship's mast and yard, the yoke of a plow, the handle of a spade, the nose and eyebrows of the human face, and so on.

"If any man will come after me, let him deny himself and take up his cross and follow Me."

With these words the cross took on a new and glorious meaning. The symbol of Death became the symbol of Life.

§ 8

The *Via Dolorosa* was mercifully short—scarcely a thousand paces. It lay from the praetorium to the Gate Genath. Outside this gate, and a few yards from the city wall beside the main road into Jerusalem from the north, stood a place called Golgotha, the Place of a Skull. There is nothing in any of the four Gospels to suggest that Golgotha was a hill, but it has been assumed that it must have been so.

Those who thronged the streets near the praetorium would have seen the terrible, but familiar, procession of muezzin - cryer of the hour of prayer

Nisan - Apr.

piaster - nickel coin. 7¢

pilchard, - fish whose young
     are sardines

Gergesa, Gergesenes

architrave - molding above column

basalt, dark marble

maniple, part of a legion of soldiers

Decapolis, district, north of Palestine,
     east and west of Jordan.

death. A centurion in charge of a half maniple of the Twelfth Legion came first, riding on horseback and clearing a path through the narrow streets. Behind him walked a legionary bearing a notice board on a pole. Written in red on a background of white gypsum was a brief account of the crimes committed by those about to die.

Jesus followed, bearing His cross beam, clothed no longer in the scarlet gown of the mockery but, as St. Matthew tells us, in His own raiment. There is an old tradition that He wore a black robe girded at the waist with a leather belt and that under it was the rich vestment given to Him in derision by Herod. He did not wear the crown of thorns, which was carried by one of the executioners in order that He might be crowned again on the cross. Worn out with suffering and with emotion, our Lord was unable to keep pace with the procession, and it seems that in the pressing into service of Simon, the Cyrenian, we may detect a touch of kindness on the part of the centurion, Longinus, who was soon to testify to the Divinity of his Prisoner and to embrace the Christian faith.

The two thieves followed, bearing the cross beams; and behind them, marching six to the rank, came the remainder of the half maniple, spear on shoulder. The Sanhedrists, who wished no doubt to enjoy their triumph, followed at the end of the procession, but, when they came to the Gate Genath, kicked their white mules into a canter and went on ahead to Golgotha.

In the sunlight of a spring morning, when the swifts were flying above the walls of Jerusalem, as they do to this day in the month of Nisan, three crosses were set up outside the city gate. Those who were "looking on afar off" covered their eyes and stood with breaking hearts. And the hours wore on. The soldiers beneath the Cross shook dice in a helmet for the seamless coat. They lay down on Golgotha in the heat of the day to eat bread and cheese and to drink their sour wine. They heard the Divine words of compassion break from the lips of the Lonely Man:

"Father, forgive them; for they know not what they do."

At three o'clock in the afternoon the Sanhedrists went to Pilate to demand the *crurifragium* in order that the bodies might not hang on the cross until the evening, which also was—how little they knew it—the beginning of a new day. And the soldiers hastened the death of the two thieves, "but when they came to Jesus, and saw that he was dead already, they brake not his legs."

.   .   .   .

The night before I left Jerusalem I went out into the streets of the old city. It was a lovely night and the moon was rising. Behind the Damascus Gate a flight of steps goes up to the city wall. Mounting the ramparts, I walked in the direction of Herod's Gate along the narrow path made for the bowmen of the Middle Ages.

The moon rose, steeping the city in a fall of light. A breathless silence lay over Jerusalem. Each dome, tower and minaret was clearly etched against the sky; each tree stood in its own small pool of moonlight. Sometimes the sentry walk descended by steps to a lower level and mounted again; sometimes I entered guardhouses set at intervals on the wall, small stone chambers through whose bow slits I saw a narrow vision of the moonlit roads beyond the city. Crossing Herod's Gate, I came at length to the corner tower and, turning to the south, walked along the east wall that overlooks the Mount of Olives.

The moon hung above the Mount, touching the ridge with a gold haze, washing every white track in light, painting each olive tree in shadow against the rocks. How hushed it was in the light of the moon. Not a footstep rang in the streets below me; no one moved in the silence beyond the wall. Above the black shadow of the Kedron Valley I could see the moonlight silvering the trees in the Garden of Gethsemane. . . .

Upon the third day, early in the morning, Mary Magdalene hastened to the Tomb, and when she saw that it was empty sorrow filled her heart, so that, St. John tells us, she wept. As she turned to go, Someone stood before her, and she heard a Voice asking:

"Woman, why weepest thou? whom seekest thou?"

"Sir, if thou have borne him hence," she begged, "tell me where thou hast laid him, and I will take him away."

"Mary."

"Master!"

Jesus instantly exhibited the strange difference that is noticeable in all his subsequent contact with the Apostles:

"Touch me not," He said gently, "for I am not yet ascended to my Father."

One imagines that Mary in her joy had flung herself at the feet of Christ and had tried to touch Him.

"Go to my brethren," He commanded, "and say unto them I ascend unto my Father, and your Father; and to my God and your God."

In the grayness of the morning the woman ran back with the message that Christ had Risen.

THE END

INDEX